Protection Spells

Spells

Tips and Tricks to Defend Yourself Against Negative Energies, Magical Attacks, and to embrace your positive power

Astrid Boe

Protection Spells

Written by Astrid Boe

Limited Liability

Please note that the content of this book is based on personal experience and various information sources, and it is only for personal use.

Please note the information contained within this document is for educational and entertainment purposes only and no warranties of any kind are declared or implied.

Readers acknowledge that the author is not engaging in the rendering of legal, financial or professional advice. Please consult a licensed professional before attempting any techniques outlined in this book.

Nothing in this book is intended to replace common sense or legal accounting, or professional advice and is meant only to inform.

Your particular circumstances may not be suited to the example illustrated in this book; in fact, they likely will not be.

You should use the information in this book at your own risk. The reader is responsible for his or her actions.

The information provided herein is stated to be truthful and consistent, in that any liability, in terms of inattention or otherwise, by any usage or abuse of any policies, processes, or directions contained within is the solitary and utter responsibility of the recipient reader.

By reading this book, the reader agrees that under no circumstances is the author responsible for any losses, direct or indirect, which are incurred as a result of the use of the information contained within this document, including, but not limited to, errors, omissions, or inaccuracies.

About the Author

Astrid Boe's story is one of cultural fusion and magical exploration. Born to an American father and Swedish mother in the coastal city of Gothenburg, Sweden, Astrid is a psychology graduate and a true devotee of the mystical arts.

Astrid's passion for nature has been a constant throughout her life, leading her to earn a degree in natural sciences. But it was during a life-changing trip to South Dakota that she discovered the shamanic culture that would shape her destiny forever.

Since then, Astrid has dedicated herself to studying and practicing witchcraft with a fervor unmatched by most. Her knowledge and experience are unparalleled, and she's eager to share them with the world through her writing.

Astrid's ultimate goal is to make the secrets of the magical arts accessible to all. Through her books, she aims to inspire and empower others to tap into their inner magic and unleash their full potential.

Table of Contents

Introduction

Protection spells may be quite beneficial, whether you're looking to safeguard your mental health, boost your self-esteem, or just find some calm in a difficult circumstance. Insecurity weighs heavily on your mind and depletes your vitality, yet the spells in this book may help you restore your comfort and security while also healing your body and mind.

Spell crafting may provide the kind of comfort that enables you to fully relax and enjoy your life, while also increasing your sense of security and preserving your positive energy. Additionally, it may assist you in providing the same degree of protection for your family, friends, and assets.

If you wish to take control of your spiritual and physical defenses, spell crafting may be beneficial to you. Don't worry if this is your first time working with spells; Protection Spells is meant to expose you to both the idea and practice of spellcraft. This book may be used by anybody, regardless of whether they are a seasoned, professional practitioner of spell craft The spells are straightforward, and the book is intended to provide you with the information and equipment necessary to do basic magic on your own.

Chapter 1

What Is a Spell?

A spell is something you perform with purpose and awareness to bring about change on some level, and it is based on the premise that everything is linked by energy. Spells are cast by carrying out a series of symbolic activities in the physical world in order to effect change on a deeper level. It seeks to influence a situation by adding new energy or dispersing energy that is already there.

When you perform a spell, you serve as a change agent, actively summoning resources to collect and direct energy. When you cast a spell, you admit that your actions are the ones that bring about change. It is your goal to initiate change, and whatever repercussions that result are also your responsibility. (More on this in the ethics sections)

How do spells work?

Everything in the world, including circumstances, has some kind of energy. All of those energies seek out to link with one another, forming a web-like network. When you use a spell to try to alter a circumstance, you change the energy in one place. That change sends shivers across the network, and every energy field ripples slightly as the energy of your spell travels to the location it intends to affect. The world is covered with these threads of energy that link everyone and everything, and it is via them that you may direct some energies toward a goal or draw certain energies toward you.

The most important part of a spell is YOU.

What causes a spell to work?

The participation of you, your will, and your goal distinguishes spells from chemistry and cookery. You are a change agent. Your action increases the energy. The movement of the energy is determined by your intent. Your aim drives it to make the changes you want.

Is it instantly effective?

No. Once you've cast a spell, you must be convinced that the change you want has already started and will be completed shortly. Then keep an eye out for and be conscious of change. It is unknown when that transformation will occur. It may sneak in gradually until one day you notice something is different and you're not sure when it began; it's simply the new normal. Changes are seldom so evident and dramatic.

Why you need to cast spells?

Everyone may benefit from stronger safeguards; safety is critical. However, there may be instances when you feel especially exposed and want to fortify your defenses.

Do you seem to be having a string of poor luck?

Are you feeling overwhelmed by feelings or pain that you can't quite put your finger on, or are you experiencing exceptionally vivid or distressing dreams? These are all symptoms that negativity is clogging up your own energy or the settings in which you work.

It's also usual to become more conscious of various energies as you begin to work with spells. After all, spell work is all about manipulating energy, and the more you practice it, the better you are at detecting, reading, and moving energy.

Your new awareness might make you feel as though all of your senses are on high alert, which can be overwhelming. Don't think you're under assault; you're merely processing through all the new information you're getting.

Here are some strategies to help you adjust to your increased level of awareness:

Work on centering and grounding.

Spend some time in nature.

Get some exercise to help you concentrate on your body and balance out the new energy awareness.

Keep a journal. Keep note of everything you're feeling and the spell work you're doing to see if there's any type of link.

Perform magical rituals on a regular basis to purify yourself and your living place in order to lessen the quantity of energy interference.

Be gentle with yourself and the process.

Casting

Here are some essential things to keep in mind while casting:

• It is critical to conduct each activity with purpose and to imagine your objective while doing so. This strengthens the energy you're gathering and codes it for your particular objective. Remember that spells don't work because you mix two herbs and a stone together; they work because you're employing materials related with your aim to assist energies your will and purpose.

• Before you begin, make sure you have all of the required items. Nothing disrupts magic and concentration more than having to stand up in the midst of a spell to retrieve a lighter or a pair of scissors. If this occurs, just pause and resume your work at a later time.

• To reduce distraction, turn off your phone and lock your door. If you can't block out the ambient noise, consider putting on headphones and listening to quiet music to get you into the mindset you need for whatever spell work you're performing.

• Determine if you need a defined circle or whether your spell may be performed without one.

Spell Classifications

You'll come across a range of spell work methods in this book. Here's a quick rundown of the many approaches you'll come across so you'll be prepared when they appear.

AMULETS

An amulet is a passive item that you carry or wear that has the capacity to ward or defend you. If you feel uneasy or vulnerable when you aren't wearing a beloved bracelet, necklace, pendant, or ring, that piece of jeweler is already an amulet: it defines a portion of your energy and you identify it with your sense of self.

The last example is an amulet that has developed simply because you carry it or wear it often, and it has become a part of you. When intentionally designing an amulet, you may base your decisions on the object's symbol or traditional connotations, your own associations with it, the form and color, and the material used to manufacture it.

BAGS WITH CHARM

Charm bags are little pouches containing things or materials that have been collected and charged for a certain purpose. Talisman bags, gris-gris bags, conjure bags, and mojo bags are some of the other names for them. A comparable function is served by a Native American medicine bag. The bag contains a range of artifacts that represent the individual's own medicine or energy, or that help to correct an imbalance or deficiency in his or her energy at the moment.

A charm bag may be generic, meant to assist your energies in general, or targeted to a particular application, such as good health, protection against bad luck, and so on. Unlike an amulet, which acts as a deterrent, charm bags and talismans actively attract things to you.

KNOT AND CORD

Once upon a time, seafarers carried knotted ropes fashioned by witches. When they required wind, they would untie a knot, unleashing the power contained therein. Knots are an excellent technique to conduct magic ahead of time and keep it ready to be unleashed when required.

Cotton, silk, wool, and linen are excellent choices. Avoid using nylon and acrylic. Of course, you don't have to use cord at all; you may do not spell using yarn, embroidery floss, tapestry wool, and strips of material. Cord magic may be defined as any kind of string making, thus whether you knit, crochet, needlepoint, or weave, you can use those abilities to cord magic.

CANDLE

Candle magic is one of the most popular forms of spells, and it's easy to see why. Candles are simple to get and utilize. Candle magic is incredibly adaptable and may be tailored to your own need. You may visualize an impediment melting away like a candle burns down, or the energy you've endowed it with being freed to accomplish its task. You might also imagine your objective being dragged toward you as the wax melts away.

You may use any kind of candle. Because they burn rapidly, tea lights and birthday candles are great. Hold a fresh candle that hasn't been used for a particular reason in your hands, think deeply about your wish or need, and then light it. Make sure you have a clear aim or end in mind; don't walk in circles around the problem. The clearer your vision of the objective, the more successful it will be.

EMPOWERING AND CHARGING

Charging and empowering are terms used to describe the process of preparing an item or component for use in a spell. Essentially, it involves imprinting your clearly stated purpose onto the thing with your own energy guided by your willpower. In the case of candle magic, you are energizing the candle with your desire or command.

SYMPATHETIC

Sympathetic magic is more of a categorization than a method. Whatever occurs to an object representing someone or something else will likewise happen to the thing or person being represented, according to sympathetic magic. A voodoo doll is an excellent illustration of sympathetic magic. It's also known as imitative magic, and it works on the principle of correspondence between the circumstance being portrayed and the portrayal itself. The item or person you're striving to protect will be the topic of your representation in protection spells.

CONTAGIOUS

Another categorization is contagious magic. Someone or anything touching a charged or charmed item in order to absorb its attributes exemplifies contagious magic. It also works in the other direction; anything that came into touch with a person or object may retain traces of its energy and can then be utilized in magic to affect it. This includes things like a footprint or a piece of clothing; similarly, the age-old notion of utilizing someone's hair or nail clippings is an example of infectious magic. When items are separated, they may be utilized as a link after they are reconnected or matched. Another kind of infectious magic is BFF necklaces, in which a pendant is snapped in half and each buddy wears half. The halves of the pendant join the two persons, much as friendship connects them.

AFFIRMATIONS

Word magic is a straightforward method of casting spells. The simplest approach to employ word magic is to speak loudly, wording your magic in an active manner, and declaring your desired reality as already accomplished. For instance, rather of stating, "I shall be bold," say, "I am brave."

Affirmations may be a very effective type of word magic. Repetition is a technique for creating a new world. They're very beneficial for changing one's mind about anything.

Affirmations are excellent for working to safeguard wealth and financial conditions, as well as for self-esteem and confidence concerns, extending awareness, and improving intuition, all of which lead to greater self-defense.

Affirmations, like other forms of word magic, should always be delivered in the present tense and in positive words. "I am secure" communicates to your subconscious mind that you are protected right now and all you have to do is recognize it, but "I will be safe" communicates to your subconscious mind that your safety will always be somewhere in the future, never now. "I'm not afraid" doesn't work as well as "I am brave," mostly because your mind focuses on the primary notion of fear rather than the negativity that comes with it.

The written form is another part of word magic. It is simple to do written magic. Take a fresh sheet of paper, whichever size you wish, and write down your desire or statement. You can fold it and burn it, wrap it up and tie a thread around it to carry as a talisman, or fold it and tuck it into a locket. Colored paper may be used to provide another degree of energy, as can colored inks or patterned paper from a craft shop in a theme that supports the purpose of your spell. The options are limitless.

Writing something out repeatedly, like saying something out loud, is another physical reinforcement of the energy of a notion. Both make use of physical activity to emphasize a mental notion. Carving phrases on a candle, writing essential words on a slip of paper to carry as a talisman or amulet, or producing a piece of magical art to exhibit in your house are all examples of written magic.

VERIFY THE POSITIVE

Affirmations are positive remarks, but the notion of creating a new reality applies to negative comments as well. If you consistently make negative comments about yourself or believe the awful things people say about you, you will create a reality that you do not desire. The term affirmation itself conveys the positive aspect of this practice. You confirm or support the new reality you want to create.

How To Do a Spell

While research has never found proof for the outcome of spells and magic, many studies of esoteric science, witchcraft, and other arts consider that spells may channel unseen forces to fulfill purposes. Whether for love, success, spiritual development, or vengeance, spells use symbolism, unique materials, spoken spells, the positions of the celestial bodies, focus, and confidence in rituals to bring your wishes to fruition.

Method 1

The Foundations of a Spell

1.

Purify oneself before casting any spell. Before trying to practice magic, it is vital to cleanse your body and mind of any doubts, devils, or spiritual pollutants that might distract you or jeopardize the spell. Purifying oneself should, in theory, be a ritual in and of itself; you should leave your body calm and your mind uncluttered.

• Soak in a bath. Take a lengthy bath, thoroughly cleanse your skin, and relax your muscles.

Dress appropriately. Put on any clothing or any special items that you have for performing magic. You're pleading with the holy powers, so dress with respect. When no one else is present, some Wicca practitioners practice naked magic ceremonies.

• Meditate till you have a clear mind. Take several deep breaths to refocus your concentration and clear your mind of distracting ideas.

• Apply suitable oils on your body. Different essential oils have a variety of uses, so if you locate one that seems to be a good fit for you, dab some on your forehead and, if desired, on your hands, hair, face, and even your chest.

2.

Purify the surrounding surroundings. If you want to operate indoors, ensure that you are not interrupted and that the area in which you intend to perform the spell is clean. As you clean, see bad energy being driven out along with distractions.

3.

Construct a circle or an altar. You must execute your ritual in a consecrated place. This may be a protective circle that shields you from ghosts and harmful energies, as well as an altar dedicated to a specific god, element, or a mix of the two. The ceremony may be performed inside the circle or in front of the altar.

• As you draw, see the protecting energy emanating from your arm, enclosing the circle in a bubble of light.

• Construct a little elevated platform on which to set a god figurine or any other symbolic depiction of the divine. It does not have to be elaborate: a stack of books will suffice as long as they are treated with regard. Consider include candles, crystals, incense, or a few objects that have spiritual significance for you, such as a modest heirloom or your spell book.

4.

Invoke the gods. Invoke a higher power verbally to bless your magic. It might be a generic prayer asking for the assistance of some power or divinity, or something particular to this spell that you have prepared. Additionally, gestures, music, dances, the ceremonial lighting of candles, or the placement of items may be included in your invocation.

5.

Consider the target of your spell and see the light pouring from you to it. When a desire is visualized, it becomes a reality.

6.

Read the spell aloud. Write a brief rhyme explaining your desire and requesting that it be granted for each spell. It does not have to be rhymed, but alliteration, cadences, rhymes, and other poetic structures may assist you in focusing on and remembering it. [2] As you picture the spell, spell it out clearly and firmly.

7.

Concluding the rite. A good spell should have a "trigger" element, which is a symbol of your readiness to join the cosmos. Tear or burn a piece of paper with your desire inscribed on it (or a sign representing your wish); toss a stone or symbolic item; light a candle with snuff; or pour or drink a potion.

8.

Say a prayer of appreciation and then tidy up. Express gratitude to any particular deities invoked. Visualize the extra energy returning to the earth by envisioning it flowing through it. Clear the circle if required and dismantle the altar if you do not want to use it immediately. Take stock of your tools and exit the room. Your spell has come to an end.

Consider doing something commonplace, such as eating, and then returning to yourself.

Method 2

<u>Considerations of the Occult</u>

1.

For instance, a spell wishing for a fresh beginning should be performed when the moon is waxing in order for the desire to come true when the moon is full. A little occult study can assist you in determining the optimal time for spells.

2.

Color-coordinate your outfit. Colors have a variety of symbolic implications in many magical systems. Once you've determined their significance, choose a color or two to complement your spell and conduct the ceremony using colored candles or crystals.

3.

Utilize herbs, oils, stones, and other natural elements. For seasoned occultists, each of these ingredients has a magical significance. Visit a new age store and get the ingredients needed to energies your spells.

4.

It is a reminder of the higher forces' beneficence. Numerous occultists invoke a variety of various gods and religious figures to assist them in their job. Develop a system of spiritual symbols that is effective for you and include it into your spells. Be advised, though, that some of these spirits have their own agendas and may attempt to alter your intentions if you are unable to control them.

5.

Possess faith. Casting a spell is just channeling your mental efforts toward a certain aim. Even if nothing supernatural occurs as a result of the spell, it enables you to clearly define your objective, and ritualizing it may help you concentrate, gain confidence, and motivate you to work harder to accomplish it.

Method 3

The Conchiglie's spell

1.

In shallow water, look for a shell. He grabs it and thoroughly dries it. This is a straightforward magic formula for granting a basic request. Utilize it to send your prayer into the cosmos, requesting the seas and the moon's power to assist you.

2.

Select or design a symbol representing your wish and adhere it to the shell. Additionally, you may design it or search for other symbols associated with the subject of your interest (love, family, health, success and so on). Draw on the shell's surface using chalk, charcoal, or any water-soluble medium.

3.

Arrange the shell along the sea or lake's edge. Place it in a location where the waves may sweep the shell away when the tide rises. The sign must face upward, towards the direction of the moon.

Utilize the crescent moon to acquire something and the declining moon to dispose of something.

4.

In the sand, create a triangle. The shell should be placed in the triangle's center.

Within the triangle, you may create significant sentences and words on the sand. Alternatively, you may manually write them on the shell.

5.

While facing the moon, recite this spell. Concentrate on your goal and attempt to say the spell reverently and with conviction.

Moon, Earth, and Sea Goddess

Each request made in Your honor must come true.

The Tides' Powers and Forces

Now it is up to your waves to invoke, and my spell to accept.

6.

Leave the place believing that your request will be granted. When the tide comes in, the inscription on the shell should be washed away, and your request should be granted by the universe, the Great One, or whichever god you believe in. Within 7-28 days, you should see a difference.

Why Your Spell is Not Working

Despite our best efforts and theoretical understanding, a spell does not always operate as we want it to. Otherwise, it is ineffective.

We'll look at 10 factors that might cause our magical effort to fail in the following sections.

Perhaps you should reconsider!

If you seek advice from a "fellow" online or from another "colleague," and even the witch who is more prone to curses disapproves of the spell you are going to do, you should probably avoid doing so. Nobody should be moralized, but you should always strive to consider the ethical reasons why your spell may not succeed.

Always keep in mind the sort of spell you want to cast and the result you want to achieve: if you want to cast a spell to deliver justice, make sure you are on the right side; if you want to win the game, wager on modest bets rather than a large lottery. If you cast a morally repugnant spell, do not protest, "There is no magic, my spell does not work!"

You haven't completed all of your responsibilities.

If you remain indoors and never meet anybody, or if you refuse to utilize dating apps, no love spell will work. If you do an unlawful act and leave a written confession to the authorities, no protective spell can rescue you. Even though it appears clear, we don't always pay attention to these little details, believing that a spell may succeed despite our "Muggle" attempts.

The improper ingredients or the phase of the moon

There are spells that operate regardless of the phase of the moon; some may even function if we are on a declining moon rather than a full moon, with no negative consequences. Finally, some avoid working or risk reprisal while the moon is in the incorrect phase. Organizing your spells according to the moon phase for the target will increase their potency. I understand that you don't always have the luxury of waiting for the proper moment, but consider the potential consequences.

Nothing will happen at all!

You really want to perform lovely magic you discovered online, but you lack all of the required elements. Should I wait or attempt to find another solution? If you require a rose for love magic but only have a chilly pepper, don't use it! Chili is sometimes employed in distance spells and curses, which might explain why the spell fails.

However, you may feel compelled to replace certain phrases or rhymes in order to hear a more "personal" spell. This is permissible as long as the purpose or structure of the document is not altered. I've changed numerous Diana invocations to make them more personal to myself.

Incorrect goal

Your spell's success might be jeopardized if you have the incorrect purpose in mind. Instead of performing a money magic, attempt to specify why you want it: maybe employment possibilities, presents, and half-price offers will arrive instead of cash!

Also, attempt to break your ultimate aim into segments, keeping in mind that it is simpler to do something basic and "little" than something excessively large. If you want to win an Oscar, enroll in an acting class and then cast a good luck magic. When casting a love spell, it is preferable to concentrate on the sort of person you desire next to you rather than on a particular individual. Maybe the person you're looking for isn't who you believe he or she is!

There is a lack of required momentum.

You have all of the necessary components, the right moon phase, and you have taken the time to meticulously prepare everything. However, it was ineffective. Because? There might be a lack of momentum for a spell to function successfully - are you certain you're performing it for the correct reason? We often feel we desire something just because society does. Graduation, marriage, children, and finding stable employment All of these things are desirable, but are they really the wants of each individual? Our unconscious understands exactly what we want, and a spell that does not represent our true wishes will often fail. Before doing any magical activity, it is important to be clear about our true objectives.

We are not paying attention or are using the incorrect strategy.

Concentration and the proper "mindset" assist us in reaching our objective. Wearing a certain outfit, having a calming herbal tea, and taking a hot bath might all be fantastic foreplay to get us in the right frame of mind for our magical job. On the contrary, doing everything in a rush, with a rush to complete, and without any precise preparation leads to the failure of our spell.

The form of a spell is determined by how all of its components are assembled. Ingredients, phrases, and gestures: each of these components is designed to amplify the appeal. If the spell is for another person, there is no purpose in constructing a bag with protection herbs to fend off harmful energy or enchanting an item we carry. The right form of a ritual seems simple enough to grasp, yet the spell often fails due to excitement for magical activity or a lack of expertise.

Our holy area is a mess.

The environment in which we cast our spell might also have an impact on its performance. A cluttered, filthy room full of stuff not ours, loud music, or the phone constantly ringing may all contribute to the collapse of our spell. Making a peaceful and clean setting, purifying it with incense, or going around the perimeter with a smudge, can aid in the spread of beneficial energy throughout the Universe.

If you don't know how to make a smudge, I will explain how below

Our target is guarded, or we lack spiritual backing.

Have you performed a ritual to assist a friend or to cast a curse on someone, but the spell did not operate as expected? The topic may be shielded. Those who perform magic often construct protective barriers around themselves or their homes in order to shield themselves from harmful energies or outside intervention. It might also be a Muggle who has elected to grow protecting herbs in the garden, perhaps as a family custom. Furthermore, even if the protection is good, there may be protections from spirits or deceased persons linked to the person on whom you are doing the spell. If you are doing protection, healing, or good luck magic, it is a good idea to notify the person involved. If, on the other hand, you have opted to cast a curse, be aware that if the spell does not work for one of the aforementioned reasons or takes much longer to take effect, you will be disappointed.

Seek spiritual assistance

Finally, for the effectiveness of our spell, it is occasionally necessary to seek spiritual assistance. Let us remember to leave an offer or something in return when we turn to a god for help with the magical task we are about to do. If we see that our spell isn't functioning, it's possible that we've called the incorrect Divinity or that we've summoned opposing forces.

What Are Freezing Spells and Why Do They Exist?

In this section, we will discuss freezing spells and explain what they are, as well as how we might employ them.

When we think of freezing, we instantly think of anything that needs to be cooled or something that needs to be paralyzed by the cold.

Cold is related with lack of emotion; a cold person is not easily stirred and finds it difficult to communicate their feelings. So, we might argue, coldness is a human attribute associated with a form of vibration in which the emotional field is less prevalent but the mental field is more present.

We are applying a power that inhibits such emotions from acting in both a circumstance and a person by conducting a calm or frozen spell.

As they normally say, it would be like applying cold clothes

It's also worth noting that during freezing episodes, there's always the chance of defrosting a person or circumstance. That is to say, it is not something we do and it stays with us forever, but it is possible to undo what we have done.

These spells are often employed for love affairs, but they may also be utilized in instances when we need something or someone to quit troubling us. That is to say, we may use this form of magic to put a halt to the energy that is entering us.

Freezing, like energy shields, is a sort of barrier or method of protection from unpleasant events or individuals.

It is also true that a freeze may be used to an internal feeling that is unpleasant for us; in this regard, it varies from the shield.

Some questions you may have concerned this subject include:

Is it possible to cast a freezing spell?

These spells may be performed by anybody who follows the instructions. What is required is a clear goal and the ability to follow the procedures outlined in the spell's instructions.

It is also vital to note that while doing this sort of magic, one must be devoid of jealousy or resentment, since the goal is to restrict external energy while avoiding creating any new type of conflict.

Negative energies tend to attract what they desire to reject; thus, you must purify your emotional body and mind in some manner before executing such a spell.

Every day, we must practice raising our vibration, which means being free of bitterness, jealously, and negativity. There are several meditations that can be done about it, and they are highly advised in order to appropriately do the freezing spell and make it work.

The most significant disadvantage of performing this sort of spell is the energy of rage that develops as a result of having to cope with the confinement of a person or circumstance. As a result, it is critical to be free of this inherent rage. To be rid of this anguish, we must trust and believe that the spell we will make will have positive outcomes.

Is it possible to freeze someone or a circumstance, or is this simply a myth?

As previously stated, the concept of freezing is linked to the concept of the brake. And it is possible to freeze someone or anything by performing a ceremony in which this principle is used to apply a sort of energy that paralyzes the active energy that seeks to interfere in our lives.

Any spell or ritual produces a unique form of energy. In this scenario, it is to develop a contrary energy that keeps the active energy from operating (when there is an active energy attempting to damage us). As a result, we've equated this period to cold sponging. Actually, we're going to use the freezing spell to generate one form of energy that paralyzes another.

The spell summons a slew of powers opposing to the force that wishes to harm you or that you want to expel from your life.

This method is sometimes performed mentally, without the need of spells. We simply remove someone from our thoughts and emotions, producing a form of frequency in which we do not allow that person or scenario to come near.

The freezing spell is an extension of this mental technique in which we assist ourselves with objects and phrases that make the energy more exact and tangible.

What are freezing spells and why do they exist?

The standard approach for a cold spell

There are key aspects that are shared by all freezing spells and rituals. For starters, ice or another form of substance that facilitates freezing is nearly always used.

In certain areas, such as warmer climates, earth, as well as a sort of combination, such as concrete, is employed as an ingredient that causes a situation or person to freeze.

In addition to these components, we need anything related to the scenario or person we wish to freeze. If it is a person, this element may be a picture; if it is a scenario, it is required to record what happened on a sheet, and the two variables, namely the sheet and the image, are often employed.

There are freezing spells or rituals that make use of anything about the person we desire to freeze, such as their hair or clothes.

When it comes to ice, the refrigerator is virtually always utilized.

Freezing spells can include terms that allude to the situation that is being frozen. Depending on the spell, these phrases might be extremely lengthy or very brief.

It is feasible to utilize one or more candles in many circumstances, although this is not a must.

As previously stated, this sort of magic may be reversed. In other words, a frozen condition may be converted into a thawing scenario.

Occasionally, re-casting the spell to thaw the situation or person is required; but, in other circumstances, thawing is done simply by removing the item symbolizing the person or scenario from the refrigerator or area where it was frozen.

A few guidelines to consider while crafting a decent freezing spell

Never be angry with the person or scenario we are going to freeze: It is critical that we can erase any negative feelings we have regarding the person or situation we are about to freeze. If there is rage, envy, or any other restless feeling, it might interfere with the spell and cause it to fail.

Prevent another person from seeing the frozen thing: because the refrigerator is normally not used for freezing spells or rituals, it is difficult to prevent others from seeing the object inside your refrigerator if you live with others. When you performed the magic, it was put there. This item must not be seen by others; thus, we propose that you disguise it by placing it inside anything that cannot be opened or identified. This is critical. The components used in any rituals or spells are not to be viewed or discussed by others, and this is especially vital in the case of a freezing spell.

Do not inform anybody that you are about to do a freezing spell - this is very crucial, since if we tell someone that we are going to perform this sort of magic, it is likely that this person may interfere in some way with our thoughts or purpose. Since a general rule, spells and rituals are not announced; nevertheless, in the instance of a freeze, it is critical that no one knows, as this is a pretty unique form of magic, so be cautious not to tell anybody. You should keep what you are doing to yourself, regardless of how trustworthy the individual is.

Choose high quality components: this is a general suggestion for every spell, but in this instance, we must be extra careful and use only the finest materials. If freezing involves a picture, make it the best you can acquire from the person you wish to freeze; if a candle is involved in the spell, make it the finest you can get.

A freezing spell is an example of a spell.

This is simply an example, but you may utilize it if necessary.

It's quite easy, and you don't even need a picture of the person you want to freeze.

This spell is great for freezing a bothersome individual or someone you no longer want to see or need to eliminate from your life. It is not applicable in certain circumstances.

A white sheet, a pen, a white candle, a plastic cup (which may be an old container), a tablespoon of soil, and a glass of water are required.

You light the white candle in front of the table and speak the following words: "By means of this spell, I will freeze this person (you state his name) and he cannot approach me, think about me, or connect to me."

Then you set the paper in front of the candle and write the name of the person you wish to freeze seven times. You must put his first and last name, separated by commas.

Then fold the paper in four, leaving the text within. Place the folded paper in the bottom of the plastic cup, followed by a teaspoon of soil.

By doing so, you are saying: "Through this land, it has covered everything that is ancient, I have closed all that is new, I have prevented whatever (name and surname) I desire."

Then, gently pour the water into the plastic cup, attempting to bring the paper to the bottom. After that, we put the plastic cup in the refrigerator. "I freeze you, and you remain frozen, until I decide to get you out of here," you say aloud.

This is an extremely strong freezing spell that may be performed when we need someone to leave us alone.

As the example above shows, freezing spells are simple to cast.

Almost often, a refrigerator is required.

It is critical not to get enraged with the circumstance or person we want to freeze.

This sort of spell is especially effective when someone demands on us or when we wish to distance ourselves from an old love.

Chapter 2

Protection Spells

In psychic self-defense, protection spells remove and reject any malicious energy bonded to or aimed against you. A protection spell might help you regain confidence while offering a psychological barrier.

Aura-cleansing/purification spells and protection spells may sometimes overlap. Some of the greatest abilities, like rosemary or salt, can do both. What spell do you need? In general, cleaning spells restore mental energy while protective spells produce a spiritual barrier that deflects external threats.

As in:

You've just seen a terrifying vehicle accident. It's possible your protecting aura has been penetrated.

You're terrified of getting into a vehicle accident, so take precautions instead of or in addition to a cleansing ceremony.

Many psychic practitioners see protection and purifying spells as complementary measures to maximizing personal power.

Psychic Bodyguard Dream Pillow Stuffing

This pillow is like having a fairy-tale brother and sister watching over you as you sleep.

Mug wort, dried, 4 l

4 oz. dry St. John's

Miniature silver coin

Bath Salts

1/2 cup bake soda

2 c. salt

Add to your bath. Add essential oils or finely powdered herbs as desired. The sea salt is the crucial component; remove the baking soda if you like, or use Epsom salts if you're feeling achy. Salt, like olive oil, wine, honey, and essential oils, is unique to its region of origin. Experiment.

Bath salt for ex

4 drops peppermint oil

4 vetiver essential oil

2 drops cinnamon oil

2 ml ginger essential oil

1 cup salt

Mix in the essential oils with the salt. These salts may tickle; unsuitable for delicate skin. Extra Protection Salts may be used as a protective floor sprinkle as well as a bath additive.

This is one of the most powerful protective cleaners. A basic salt and oil combination becomes a sensual medium. Even if you disbelieve its magical powers, this product will leave your skin feeling revitalized and invigorated. Gently massage the salt into your skin; picture your objectives and repeat your affirmations.

Scrubs

1 cup salt

1/2 cup oil

Put salt in an airtight container (Mason jars are great). 12 cup high grade oil the best consistency is safflower oil, but I've also used sweet almond oil. Mix the oil and salt till desired consistency. The softer the scrub, the more it exfoliates and leaves you feeling thoroughly cleaned, spiritually and physically.

Add essential oils for intensification or extra magical purposes. When the mixture reaches the proper consistency, add the essential oils, a few drops at a time, mixing well. For numerous wants, just blend different essential oils with the restriction of 10-12 drops of essential oil for 1 cup of salt. 1 tablespoon infused oil 1 cup salt

Botanical Defenses

Basil: boosts money, heals a lover's feud, and brings luck to a new business or house.

Bergamot: invites luck and wealth.

Frankincense: for spiritual protection and breaking harmful associations.

Safety Trees

Dogwood, Hawthorn, Juniper, Oak, Olive, Rowan. Arrange the trees in a circle for safety.

Gardenia: for protection against individuals bringing, your problems. (Mother-in-law scent.)

Hex-busting Geranium:

Love, romance, fertility, and better sex.

Rose: builds self-esteem and self-acceptance.

Rosemary: protect, protect, protect!

Sandalwood: protects the spirit

Ylang: promotes open communication.

St. John's Wort floral essence fosters spiritual security.

There are amulets for general protection and protective amulets for specialized purposes. Amulets for children, animals, and the house are available.

Mirrors are amulets. They are said to confound low-level malicious spirit creatures as well as reflect the Evil Eye. (Painting your ceiling blue confuses them and sends them packing!)

In China, Feng Shui is a science that studies how to arrange objects for protection, progress, and luck. The main entryway, master bedroom bed, and toilets should not be mirrored.

To fully benefit from crystals' care, you must also care for them. If your protection crystal is in use, keep it cleansed and re-charged.

Black protects psychically. Black tourmalines are the most potent of all black crystals for personal protection. Unlike other black gems, black tourmaline acts as a barrier, deflecting destructive energy.

Iron and silver are psychic protection metals.

Body

Although people typically resort to external sources for personal safety, pictures of the human body have historically provided strong protection.

Eyes

Another eye overcomes the Evil Eye. Another eye attracts the Evil Eye, preventing it from looking elsewhere, then boomerangs it, acting as a shield. A diamond, almond, or triangular form is sometimes employed, bordered by brow motifs. The brows alone may be enough to scare away the Evil Eye. Greek and Turkish blue glass eyes adorn necklaces, walls, and rear-view mirrors. They are said to operate best when given as gifts.

The color of the yarn reflects the kind of protection and power required. These amulets also bring wealth and masculine offspring. Their size varies, but they are always individualized amulets. Despite the lengthy instructions, making this amulet is simple and soothing.

God's Eye

2 dowels

Glue, scissors

2 or 3 color yarn

1. Develop a not in the center of each dowel.

2. Glue the dowels together to make a cross. It's like four-wheel spokes or four cross arms.

3. Select 1 option of yarn for the pupil and loop it around the center numerous times until it is fully covered.

4. Begin around the dowels. Begin at the 1st dowel and work clockwise around the 2nd arm, up and over the 3rd.

5. Add the second color: iris. Place it towards the inner diamond. Glue a dab (not completely authentic, but it will stay on better).

6. Always blow clockwise. Return to the 1st dowel and knot and cut the yarn.

7. Attach a third color yarn or go back to the first and construct one more diamond. (Make as many as you like.)

8. Finish your mojo by wrapping the yarn entirely around the first dowel. Trim any extra yarn. Wrap, tie, or glue the end.

9. Recover the other three arms in the same way. A pom-pom on top and yarn tassels on the dowels offer additional benefits.

Hands

Grab a hand to equip yourself with a protective amulet! Again, blue is the preferred color—have kids paint their hands blue and push them against your walls to keep an old custom alive. The Hand of Power is one of the world's oldest emblems, dating back to Paleolithic times. The Moroccan proverb "five in your eye" defends the Evil Eye. An amulet may depict a hand or five dots, lozenges, or squares. Because five represents the fingers and the strength of the hand, it is often used in protection charms.

Pre-Christian Scandinavian amulets are still popular today. The cross's form denotes protection in all directions. It's easy to build if you have the supplies.

Vinegar

2 cups white vinegar

6 tbsp chopped basil

10 gr crushed garlic

1. Pour the vinegar over the basil and garlic.

2. Cover and infuse for 3 days.

3. Strain and sterilize the liquid.

4. If desired, garnish with entire garlic cloves or basil leaves. When you need a psychological barrier, add a splash to your bath.

Protection Mix

4 drops frankincense oil

4 ml lavender essential oil

2 ml rosemary essential oil

Blend the oils and add to your bath water or massage with a cup of sweet almond oil.

Are you hoodooed? You can change it!

Bain de Cure

Angelica

Agrimony (breaks and returns hexes.)

Chamomile

Hydrangeas

Lovage

Use three dried botanicals.

Hex bath

1/2 cup coconut

a pinch salt

Lemon verbena, patchouli, lavender

1. If the coconut oil has hardened, gently heat it over low heat until it liquefies. Do not burn or overheat.

2. Stir in the salt.

3. You may now add the fragrances: herbs finely powdered (a pinch), essential oils (2 drops), or a mixture. Lemon essential oil may be replaced with a splash of lemon juice. If you prefer, add lemon zest.

4. Timed to the full moon for maximum impact.

Feet

While pictures of hands, eyes, and genitals ward off the Evil Eye, genuine feet are particularly susceptible. Humans have a mental Achilles heel on the soles of their feet. Feet aren't normally thought of as orifices, yet they may be ideal access points for healing or malicious spirits. However, footbaths are regarded excellent therapeutic venues for aromatherapy or other herbal treatments.

Test it out: rub a sliced clove of garlic on the soles of your feet and wait for the garlic flavor to emerge. For those with calloused feet, it should be quick.

Poison isn't always literal. Protective rites involving the feet really give all-around protection.

• First, henna on the soles beautifies, disinfects, prevents athlete's foot, and seals in spiritual protection.

• Alternatively, if you feel you've stepped into an unholy area, the following ritual may be helpful.

Foot Care Ritual

Mint dried

peppermint

rosemary

1 cup safflower or equivalent oil

1/2 cup salt

1/4 cup hazelnut oil

4 drops myrrh, vetiver, or patchouli

1. Combined mug wort, peppermint, and rosemary infusion.

2. Make a salt scrub using salt and vegetable oil.

3. Fill a bucket with hot water for a footbath.

4. Add the infusion and sea salt.

5. Soak your feet for 15 minutes.

6. A foot massage seals the ritual: heating a tiny bit of walnut or hazelnut oil. (Sunflower oil works well on a budget.)

7. 4 drops myrrh, patchouli, or vetiver Continuing with the soles, massage up to the ankles.

8. This practice works well shortly before night. Just get into bed (or better yet, conduct the massage in bed; your feet will be slick) and don't move for many hours.

Ankle Bracelet

This fortunate charm shields you from the inside out. The roots of Viburnum plants are called Devil's Shoestrings. They resemble threads. This small charm requires nine roots of similar length, which cannot be cut. Pick your roots wisely.

9 Devil's Shoestrings origins

a silver rings

1. Attach the silver bead or fortunate charm. Make sure the coin is real and not merely plated silver.

2. Wear the anklet for luck and protection.

Typical Voodoo pictures include a pin-sticked doll. Dolls are often utilized magically to promote romance, fertility, or healing. However, destructive stick-pins-where-you-want-it-to-hurt magic originates from the British Isles and Northern Europe and commonly involves a wax poppet. Dolls may be used to remove harm as well as inflict it.

Sender Doll Ritual

2 red flannels

Nettles

Paper and pen

Needles, pins, and scissors

1. Pin one cloth on top of the other.

2. Cut 2 cloth figurines.

3. Sew the 2 flannel pieces together, leaving a head hole (or wherever you prefer). Don't over-customize it. You're not attempting to hex someone, just return anything. Keep your poppet unassuming. Save your ingenuity for other things; nothing on the doll should remind you of you.

4. Stuff the opening with nettles (use gloves; they hurt) and stitch it up.

5. Pin a little piece of white paper to the poppet with "Return to Sender."

6. Face the doll and tell it to go.

7. Or leave it at a four-way intersection near your house.

(This spell works best with a full moon.)

Jinx Removal Ritual

Words have a life and force of their own once spoken. As sure as using ancient metaphysical secret words, telling a youngster he will never amount to anything curses him. "You're exactly like your father," "you'll never stop drinking," "no one will love you."

Poisons and curses both have antidotes. If you've been cursed in this way, whether it's now or years ago, here's a cure:

1. Write out the curse precisely as you remember it, including the embarrassing details.

2. Finish by writing CANCEL or VOID over it in huge letters. If it helps, scrawl over the old junk.

3. When you're ready, pick your element of destruction: fire or water.

- If you select water, tear the paper and flush it. Plain paper tends to float. Wait until every last piece has gone down the drain, even if this requires flushing repeatedly. Followed by methods to cleanse the toilet and your aura.
- If you use fire, burn the paper until no letters remain. Small ashes may be flushed down the sink; larger ashes can be scattered in the wind. Do not bury.

Ginger flower garlands are beautiful, romantic, and spiritually protective.

Anger Bath

Chamomile

Catnip

Lavender

Cherries flower essence 4 dips (Bach, Healing Herbs, Pegasus)

This bath may be made with either herbs or essential oils, depending on what you have on hand.

Make a fast infusion of herbs and add to a bath.

Alternatively, if you're too tired to cook, add 3 drops of each essential oil to your bath.

Put the cherry plum drops on your tongue or forehead.

If you struggle with anger management, mix the recipe (cherry plum flower essence with an herbal infusion or essential oils) with spring water and have it handy to calm down.

Skin irritant; apply to hair rather than skin.

Chapter 3

How to Spell Against the Evil Eye and Expel It?

Friday the 13th, black cats, crawling under a ladder. If being married on a Tuesday is considered bad luck in Spain, a tingle in the right hand is considered a sign of receiving a gift in India. If the list of beliefs is endless, there is one that is universal: the evil eye. Before diving into the many ways employed in various cultures to combat the evil eye, keep in mind that you may schedule a customized consultation with one of Femme Astro Consult's divinatory art professionals.

The evil eye: these "symptoms" that might serve as a warning

Evelyne Keller traces this idea all the way back to antiquity in her Encyclopedia of common fears and wisdom, 301 superstitions. "Fragments of Chaldean terracotta attest to this tradition of casting "the evil eye." A protective ritual against the evil eye was discovered on a 7th-century BC Babylonian papyrus..."

At the root of this misfortune is a person who is envious and jealous of you. This evil look thus has the potential to disrupt your whole existence. You then become a magnet for ill luck. Forgetfulness, loss, worry, or illness: the evil eye's effects might be similar to those of Mercury retrograde. The objective is to deprive you of the object of your envy. Each area of the earth has evolved its own set of ideas and tactics for self-defense throughout time. The hand of Fatima, the crimson thread, the black mark... A brief tour of the universe of spells against the evil eye.

How do the Turks fight off the evil eye?

Have you ever seen a blue eye suspended from a tree, hung at a house's entryway, or worn as a necklace? This talisman, often known as an "amulet of Nazar" or "Nazar," is ubiquitous throughout Turkey and Greece. Its primary source of protection is its color, which is often indigo blue. In these nations, as well as in Egypt, the notion is that blue is the divine's manifestation. Thus, according to custom, at a wedding, "we place or sew a blue pearl on the back of the bridal gown to safeguard it from the evil eye."

The evil eye: An Indian protective symbol

Married ladies put a crimson dot on their forehead to ward off ill luck. To bring good fortune, it is customary to toss a penny into a fountain, a well, or a river. India is a land of many superstitions. Thus, Indian moms paint a black patch on their child's face to fend off the evil eye.

Garlic's benefits against the evil eye

Rather than the legends that garlic is the finest defense against vampires, this vegetable is better renowned for its ability to fend off bad spirits. Thus, garlic is well-known throughout the Mediterranean region for its ability to ward off the evil eye. " We construct bouquets with the capex that are strung with a strand of red wool and hung in the dwellings."

Wear a hand of Fatima to fend off the evil eye.

According to the myth, if you lose it... you might lose your life! Fatma's hand, which dates all the way back to ancient Egypt and India, made its way to France through Spain and the conquering of the Moors. On home doors, around the neck, or embroidered on garments, this protective sign is seen across North Africa. In the Maghreb, it is customary to dip one's hand in green paint after "the home is whitewashed and dazzlingly white" to fend off the evil eye.

How to get rid of the evil eye in Morocco using sea water and number 7?

While it is not unusual to see individuals in Morocco clutching Fatma's hand, another notion prevails. To ward off the evil eye from a property, "you must wash the tiles seven times with seven successive wavelets" using saltwater gathered in a container.

The crimson thread serves as a deterrent to the evil eye.

Frequently referred to as Kabbalah, the red thread connects Tel Aviv and Marrakech through Estonia or Thailand. Its color is auspicious and provides good fortune. Women sew a crimson thread around the bottom of their skirts in the Estonian islands of Kahn and Manija, for example, to fend off ill luck. The red thread, which is frequently worn as a bracelet, was "repolarized" in the 1990s/2000s by celebrities. Far from fashionable, it would be one of the world's oldest amulets.

Did you know that in Japan, when a terrible forecast is drawn from the Omikuji, a divinatory oracle, the prediction must be hung on a tree to ward off the evil eye?

The efficacy of salt

"Throughout the Middle Ages and into the modern day, the Evil One was warded off using salt... salt that was formerly utilized in the Christian baptism ceremony. Alomancy, or salt divination, is the source of the superstition associated with the spilt saltcellar, which is a terrible omen." This is not, however, the sole use of this device. " Salt is also one of the oldest talismans in Kabbalah, which advocates burying it in little canvas bags in all corners of the home. " Would so protect you from ill luck.

Lemon balm, tourmaline, and the circle of protection are all witchcraft concoctions used to fend from destiny.

Warding off ill luck is not an easy feat for witches as well. Tefen-Tiana Funereal shares her magical ritual in her book Sortileges to uncover the strong feminine. Plants disclose their abilities, making them a preferred weapon of witches. To combat the evil eye, lemon balm, St. John's wort, or cinchona may be used. These three plants possess the ability to shield themselves from dangerous and bad effects. Similarly, some stones possess a defensive quality that might be beneficial. Thus, black tourmaline may function as a "barrier against the jealous and envious." Finally, the circle of protection is an essential ritual. "It is a chance to overcome negative influences, to fend off ill luck, and to change harmful habits," the author explains. Discover how to prepare it fast and witch tactics for warding off the evil eye.

Chapter 4

Protection Techniques

Like spells, tools are also made by humans. What may be important to you depends on your own traditions and needs. For Wiccans, they need an athame, but in the old Saami religion, it was the drum. The more "material" you use for ceremonial "High" magic, the more you'll need to do it.

Because so many books have been written about magic, there is often a lot of focus on tools. The magic of poor people, the magic of slaves, or the magic of light-traveling nomads is no less powerful, but it may require less, or at the very least different, equipment than the magic of rich people.

There are a lot of magical tools that show off how good humans can be and how creative they can be. Some things are only used for magic, while others look like normal household items. You should think about your own needs, preferences, and strengths, and then look for tools that speak to you, that connect with you.

Charms and Amulets

Talismans are the traditional lucky charms that bring good luck to the person who wears them. Amulets, on the other hand, usually have protective, preventative, or therapeutic properties. There is a lot of confusion because the English language likes to skim over these topics. They call each type of talisman or amulet by a very unique name in other languages. Our word "amulet" is said to come from the Latin word "amulet," which means "a way to protect" (reminiscent of ammunition).

Talismans and amulets are often broken down into two groups:

People who are made up

Self-contained things

Magical spells are used to make talismans and amulets on a regular basis.

Bells

There is a lot of magic in bells, and they have a long history and are used all over the world. They are used in a lot of spells, like the ones below:

Magic that helps you get pregnant is called a fertility spell (a bell will not "function" unless it has a clapper)

Spells that can bring spirits to you

Spells that protect you

Spells that make the environment cleaner.

A spell is a thing that helps people.

Church bells were made because they were used for magic, not the other way around.

Bells are made of many different things, but silver and iron are especially good for protection, fertility, and healing. Bells that are meant to be amulets can also be made into symbols, like pinecones, cats, and frogs, so these types of bells have been found.

People can also scrape off the grease from big bells like church bells and use it to banish or curse people.

Books

In late antiquity, there was a big rise in witchcraft, sorcery, and paganism being punished and tried for crimes. Other than astrology, divination, making love potions, and asking for help at pagan temples, one of the accusations was that he had magic books.

Books play a lot of different roles in magic, not just as a source of spells. The book itself could be a kind of magic, like a charm. Some books don't need to be read, but just having them in the house protects against a number of illnesses. Another book in this genre is called The Book of Raziel, and it isn't the Bible or the Koran.

Books are magical tools. There are many texts that can be used as divination sources. The Bible, the Koran, Homeric poems, and Virgil's writings are all in this group.

As a magical book, the Book of Psalms has a second person. Many people use psalms to do magic. There are a lot of people who think that Hoodoo started this, but this isn't true because Hoodoo doctors aren't very well-educated, so they must have made things up. In fact, the opposite is true: Psalms have been used in magic for a long time. An early compilation of possible uses for psalms and their lines was published because people were doing this a lot. When The Magical Use of the Psalms was popular, it was often reprinted in small copies and translated into different languages from Latin.

Islamic spells, on the other hand, may call for the recitation of important lines from the Koran.

Paper

Many spells have text in them. Some things must be written down, even if only to be burned down. As a result, paper must be used.

The old grimoires often say that parchment or vellum should be used when making a talisman. Because these are long-lasting, even though they may be hard to get now, they are a good choice. Hoodoo often tells people to use brown paper. Use paper bags or butcher paper that has been cut in half. It is cheap, easy to get, and has a good color because brown is the color of justice. Thus, this material makes any spell that calls for justice to be done more powerful because it has more power.

Also, it is very easy to write your own paper even if you don't have any ideas. Children's art kits come with everything they need to make basic paper. A spell is rarely longer than a piece of paper. The best thing about making your own paper is that you can add botanicals and fragrances that you like.

Broomsticks

The picture of the witch riding her broomstick is based on real events. In Western European fertility ceremonies, broomsticks were used a lot. A group of women on brooms and a group of men on pitchforks galloped across fields, leaping high in joy to help the crops grow. The pitchfork, which is a tool used by men, was later thought to be one of the devil's traits.

Because a broom is useful. It shows how the male and female energies are completely fused, with the stick representing the male power being plunged into and connected to the straw. The handfasting ceremony of leaping the broomstick still has some of the broom's fertility magic in it.

For a while, it looked a lot like a barbershop pole or pawnbroker's balls as the symbol of a midwife's job.

Broomsticks aren't just a symbol of magic in Europe. The symbol also came to be in Mexico on its own. The conquistadors were shocked to see Tazolol, the fiery Aztec spirit of love and witchcraft, riding a broomstick that was only covered in jewels and a conical bark cap.

The broom is used for many things:

It has become a symbol of witchcraft in the same way that it used to be a symbol of middle-wives. It is possible to show them off as a source of pride and as a reminder of the Burning Times.

Brooms are a kind of amulet that protects you from bad magic.

They are used in a wide range of magical spells, including spells to get rid of bad things, clean, and increase fertility.

The broomstick was used in the past to apply witches' flying ointments to the skin.

There are a lot of different types of brooms:

Single-use ceremonial brooms, which are often made of plant material and dismantled and given away right after they are used.

Special magical brooms are only used for ceremonial purposes.

A simple household broom, like the one used to sweep the floor, is an important part of Hoodoo banishing spells. Through the use of ceremonial floor washes, both spiritual and normal home cleanings can be done at the same time.

Candles

Candles are a very recent addition to magic: until recently, real candles were too expensive, which led to the popularity of lamp magic. Beeswax was hard to get, and natural plant waxes take a lot of work to make. Around 3000 BCE, we first saw what we now call a candle.

The first real candles were made with a wick made of wax, oil, or fat that hardened at room temperature. This is different from the oil lamps that were more popular in the past. Beeswax was thought of as a high-end product, on a level with sandalwood and frankincense.

Paraffin was invented, and until then, the most popular candle was made of tallow, an animal fat that was easy to find in your kitchen. The bad thing about tallow is that it smells bad. There are still a lot of Latin American magical traditions that use small tallow candles. You can often find them at spiritual supply stores.

In addition to beeswax, bayberry, and candelilla, there are a lot of beautiful natural waxes that you can use. Even though the substance is stronger and more beneficial than paraffin, it costs a lot more. If you burn candles a lot, they might be too expensive for people who do that often.

People who love figure candles may also have a hard time finding candles made with finer waxes.

Cauldrons

You might need to have a hearth, fireplace, wood-stove or bonfire near you to do some of the older spells. This is because this was important before the invention of the modern stove. However, in the twenty-first century, people living in cities may not have as much access to open fire as they used to.

Iron cauldrons that are the right size can often be used instead of a hearth or fireplace. A cauldron is a common witch's tool. It can be used to make potions, burn incense, and cook a meal.

Charm in bags

A bag with a magical spell inside. A lot of different things are made with charm bags. There are conjure bags and medicine hands. There are also gris-gris bags and orange bags. There are also gris-gris hands and plain old mojo. There are also phylacteries for people who want to learn more. It only has English names. These are by far the most common way to move magically charged things around the world.

In a charm bag, there is a pouch that holds one or more powerful things. There are some people who think of them as little magic or prayer boxes that are inside a bag. Others are works in progress: a collection of powerful things that are always changing.

Simple medicine packs can be made. If you want to protect yourself from the Evil Eye or find and keep true love, you should wear an amulet bag filled with earth from a three-way crossroads around your neck.

Also, medicine packs can be hard to figure out. If you buy a Patau, which is a Brazilian charm bag made of leather or fabric, you might find a dandelion root that looks like the fig hand. It is sandwiched between leaves of rue and Macura. To make it even better, you can add garlic and cloves, then write prayers and sew them into the bag.

Certain traditions require that you carry a lot of different things in one bag. If you start a medicine bag in Native North American tradition, you put in something that will get it going. This could be a little tobacco or pollen or maize kernels. You could also put in some white sage, white sage leaves, or Earth wrapped in red cloth. Many other traditions only need one thing in a bag. In orthodox Muslim tradition, magic is not allowed, except for the use of Koranic texts as amulets, which are allowed. Each amulet needs its own bag. It is common for African nomads to keep their luck charms in leather and metal pouches.

This kind of magic is so diverse that there is no end to it. The container is now part of the spell. A handkerchief may be all that's inside some "bags." There are a lot of different types of drawstring bags. Hoodoo says to wear red flannel, while Romany tradition says to wear red silk.

When people talk about "hands," they usually refer to closed bags, not ones that open up. If you look at the fabric used to make the two, you can tell the difference between them.

They look like a single quilt square because of the material that was sewn inside. The outside of the mojo hand is then decorated with beads.

Bags are convenient, but there are many ways to transport charms. In Romany style, the bag can be sewn into clothes, or parts of the bag can be sewn into clothes. This gives more privacy and more contact with the body.

Little balls of crystal.

Using a spell goes beyond the idea of a con artist using a crystal ball to get money. It has been used for a long time and is well-liked. As it turns out, crystal balls are a new addition to the ancient practice of scrying. Scrying is a type of divination in which mirrors are used. I think it is one of the most difficult ways to get information about the past. The transparent spherical crystal ball of the modern era is especially beautiful because it looks like the moon.

The first scryer, most likely, looked into a calm lake, like this. In Roman art, the goddess Kybele is shown with a pan of water that is flat on the bottom so that divination can happen. You can use a simple pan of water to look into the future. If you have one of these priceless jewels and want to learn how to scry, just look at the crossed lines on them and let your mind go. For communicating with spirits or ghosts, smokey quartz is said to be a very good thing to have around you.

There are times when Indians don't have water in their pans, so they use a pool of ink. Staring into a container of ink held in the left hand was part of the Egyptian process.

Unlike pans, crystal balls, like mirrors and gemstones, can keep images and memories from being lost. As needed, get rid of the dirt and grime that has built up.

The light of the autumn moon can charge crystal balls if you keep them in the light of the moon on a daily basis.

According to some people, a crystal ball must be completely charged by the light of thirteen full moons before it can be used.

If you want to use your crystal ball to connect with the spiritual world, you may want to cover it with a black cloth when you're not using it.

Dolls

They are also called "poppets," but that's not all. "Doll" is linked to the word "idol," and "poppet" is linked to the word "puppet." This is how the typical witch's doll looks like. It is made of wax and filled with pins to make the person feel pain and agony. If you want to make a magical spell doll, you can make it from a lot of different things and use it for a lot of different spells. Dolls have been made of wax, but also cloth and plants and wood and bone. They have also been made of clay.

It is possible to use dolls in positive magic to do the following things.

Cure sickness

Then, make people feel loved.

Bring back together what was lost.

Enhance and improve fertility.

On the other hand, dolls have been used to hurt people, make them impotent, kill them, make them suffer, make them crazy, and do a lot of other bad things to them.

Fabrics

Spells often need to be wrapped in cloth. The cloth is taken in by the spell. Many cultures have "holy" textiles. The way these textiles are made is often based on mystical or spiritual traditions, like batik or ikat, which are both ways to make them. They use red silk and red fleece the most when they do spell work.

Many traditional needlework techniques are linked to religious traditions. The beautiful needlework designs worn by Baltic, Hungarian, Romany, and Slavic women are thought to bring good luck, strength, protection, and fertility.

As a starting point for making magical fabrics, flags are among the most important.

Belts with Magic

From the cingulum to the waist beads, this type of magical instrument covers everything that goes around the waist or hips and is made for a magical reason. The category may have been called "girdles," which is a term that has been out of favor but was once thought of as sensual and magical: When someone is in need of love-inducing belts or girdles, Aphrodite and Ishtar both give them away. The belt is usually, but not always, used by women to perform magic. The belt isn't just about love, sex, and having kids, even though it's a woman's thing. Both Aphrodite and Ishtar have military traits. A powerful female warrior called Oya is also linked to belts, which are also made of leather. Belts are also used in powerful, protective spells for women.

Before, magic belts were a huge hit. Women were buried in Cro-Magnon tombs with cowrie shell belts. They run horizontally across the belly, which means that the person is pregnant. Amulets, such as mojo bags, are worn on the belts, and they help people do good things. If you look at belly dancers, you might find some of the belts with a lot of glitter. (Shed is the key word. It is important that the skin is not removed forcibly; the snake powers must help; fertility is a snake's gift.)

Many magical belts have a sexual element to them. People in traditional Africa thought that waist beads were a lot of fun to wear, and so they kept them private. Some of the beads are moved to the neck to make up for this.

They can also be used for public events.

Boxes full of spells

When you want to cast spells, you need to build a spell box, which is an enclosed altar or tableau. In general, a magic box has everything you need to do a job, but you should follow the instructions for each spell. It could be a cumulative spell that is done in stages. Sometimes, a unique box can be used for a mystical or spiritual reason.

Make sure the power objects, like charms, shells and beads, are attached and integrated into the box itself so that they work together.

Magic ink, henna, or other natural colors can be used to add sigils or other lucky symbols to your clothes or skin.

Milagro

One of the most common ways to make a Milagro is to make it look like a specific body part, such as the heart or the arm. These artifacts are usually linked to magic in Latin America, but they have been around for a long time. They were first used in ancient times. Items called ex-votos have been found in Greece, Italy, and Switzerland. In Latin, these things are called "ex-votos," and they were found in those places. The first are thought to have come from Iberia.

Milagros is a kind of magic that changes a lot. Most of the time, they are made of cheap silver-colored metals, but they can also be made of precious metals and gemstones, or made entirely out of wax. Milagros can be found at spiritual goods stores and through a number of Latin American art and craft importers. Milagros is often used in healing and spirit-calling rituals, as well as protection and love charms.

The pestle and mortar

People almost always have to crush something or mix together a bunch of plants at one point or another. Mortars and pestles are simple tools that have been around since the beginning of time. To start with, the instrument looks very much like a sexual act or the act of making something new. After all, what is magic but the act of making, of making? This is said in one of the less-known Greek stories. Prometheus stole fire, but another myth says that Hermes, the Opener of Ways, makes fire first by smashing the pestle in the mortar with a lot of force.

For another thing, the physical act of hand grinding allows you to make your goals a part of the botanicals.

If you don't have a mortar and pestle, you should use manual techniques instead of a food processor, even if you have one. There are two ways to do this: You can either smash or roll the material, putting the strength of metal in your hands.

The mortar and pestle are also a witch's way of getting around, which could help explain the botanical roots of flying ointments. She's a wild Russian witch and a master herbalist.

Instruments of Music

Was magic used to make certain musical instruments, or did these instruments have to be made because of a magical need? During the first magical events, music and dance were used. While a spell book can't adequately record these rituals, they are still used in healing and trance ceremonies all over the world. Music is used to perform exorcisms and communicate with God.

Sieves

People have used magic with this seemingly harmless cooking item for a long time and in a very good way. A sieve is sometimes called a riddle because it has a lot of holes in it.

The term doesn't just apply to modern metal strainers. It also refers to any type of sifter, like a grain winnow. is a case of ancient multitasking.

Sieves are now only found in kitchen cupboards, even though they were once thought of as standard magical equipment. It is important to Isis because she used it to get Osiris' limbs. There are also a lot of Gnostic-etched jewels with the sieve on them, too. Later, the Roman Catholic

Church said that Satan was behind the sign.Sieves are used in a lot of different spells, including ones for fertility, weather control, and divination.

Swords

Chinese, Japanese, Jewish, and Persian magic has used swords for a long time. Wicca, on the other hand, has used them for a very short time. Real working swords or replicas for ceremonial use can be used. The sword is made of metal, but wooden swords are also used in traditional East Asian magic.

Once upon a time, each sword was made to fit the person who was going to use it, just like a magic wand is. Crafting was done in secret. Master swordsmiths kept their formulas secret, but sometimes rumors spread that human blood was needed to make a magical sword. Japanese mythology still has some of these stories in it.

A good sword was thought to be as important as a person; each had a name, preferences, and was thought to have a personality. The legendary sword in Crouching Tiger, Hidden Dragon is made of this kind of metal.

According to Chinese tradition, the most valuable magical sword is one that comes from a well-known and successful warrior, even if it is only used for magic.

The power of the sword can be increased by adding things to it.

Swords are used in many different types of ceremonies. They are used to make circles. When swords aren't being used, they are wrapped in red silk.

Magic swords aren't always real swords. These coins swords are both a way to protect yourself and a way to balance and improve your finances.

Wands of Wonder

Because magic wands are such an integral part of depictions of fantasy magic, it is critical to emphasize that the wand does not operate; the practitioner does. The wand is only a means through which the user's desire or purpose may be directed. Clearly, some wands are superior than others; some wands are more suited to certain objectives, practitioners, or traditions than others.

Historically, magic wands have been used in a variety of magical traditions around the world. They are particularly prominent in contemporary Druidic, Wiccan, and High Ritual traditions. Wands are both a spiritual and religious ceremonial instrument and a magical tool. Certain traditions necessitate the use of a wand as a necessary magical instrument.

That being said, it should be pointed out that not everyone who does this kind of thing or does spells with wands does. Having magic doesn't have to be the case.

With wands, we enter a world of very personal magic. Some people collect wands, choosing different woods for different magical reasons. Those who want to form a close relationship are looking for one wand with which they can build that relationship. The wand is almost like a part of the body. For some people, having a beautiful, painstakingly made wand is a must.

Others like to work with branches that haven't been carved, sticks that have fallen, or driftwood.

An umbrella that can be folded up is good for outdoor events that need to be kept quiet. Make sure you treat the umbrella like a magic wand in that case.

Even though most wands are made of wood, metal wands can be very powerful.

Staff

Wands and staffs are often different because they are different in size. Staffs have been linked to ancient Egyptian and Semitic magic, as well as the Biblical Moses and his enemies in Egypt. They have also been linked to staffs.

The modern staff is most closely linked to Obeah, the West Indies' African-derived customs that are still practiced today. People also call these carved wooden sticks Obi Sticks. They have a snake-shaped design on them. The simplest ones are made in a way that makes the staff look like a snake. The more complicated Staff of Moses is often carved from the bottom to the top with a snake. Hollowed-out staffs can be filled with plants.

Magical Skills That Are Important

Bathing

It might seem like this is the magical equivalent to how to heat water, but baths are used to do a lot of different spells. Many magical techniques make a spell more likely to work.

In general, it's good to completely submerge yourself in water at least once, but some spells say how many times you need to do this.

Allow the air to dry. It's a good idea to dry yourself with a towel to get most of the residue that comes with a bath off your skin. If you take the time to air dry, you will always get stronger and better results.

What may be the oldest magic techniques, like foot track spells and knot magic, may not make sense to the person who does them now.

Enigma of the foot track

"Leave nothing but your footprints," or so eco-tourists are told today. However, even footprints have their magical purposes. If you look at the name, you can see that foot track magic is most closely linked to hoodoo today. However, it is a very old, all-encompassing magical way of thinking. The Talmud talks about it in indirect ways. Pythagoras told people not to cut into footprints with a nail or knife, even though this book has some of the same charms.

To a certain extent, men can use foot track magic because they often leave more powerful impressions on the ground than women.

For banishing or hexing, one type of foot track magic changes the physical imprint in the earth. The other type of magic, which is used for other things, doesn't change the imprint. It's also possible to pick up all the dirt from the footprint. This is often mixed with other chemicals for both good and bad magic.

When collecting footprints, it is very important to get the whole thing for the spell to work. In addition, it is very important (and not always easy) to get the right person's footprint.

Knotting

Knots have been linked to magic for a long time, so much so that tying knots was once thought of as magic in general. From Babylon to unknown history, this art has been around for a long time. Kameda, the Hebrew word for amulet, comes from the root word "to bind." The first binding spell is knotting.

There are many ways to use knots to tie or control any kind of thought or force. What makes the magical knot different from tying a shoelace is the person who makes it. It's also possible to turn tying a shoelace into a magical act: tie the shoelace of a child's sneaker, then think about blessing and protecting them as you tighten the knot,

This means that, when you tie a knot, your energy is being focused and concentrated with each knot.

It is common to use knot magic to make people fall in love, heal, make money, and change the weather. This is called "knot magic" (i.e., controlling the wind and rain).

Knots are used to connect thoughts and to get rid of spells. They are often used in art from the Celtic, Chinese, Egyptian, and Scythian cultures, as well as many other cultures. Love knot magic is where the term "lover's knot" comes from. It's said that some people believe that the ring was made with knot magic in mind.

The spider is the animal that helps with knot magic.

This is the spell for the Basic Knot.

1. Keep your goal and desire in mind while holding a red cord in your hands.

2. A knot is made.

3. If you want to keep it safe and sound, wrap it up in fabric and put it in a magic box.

The knot is used in a traditional incantation.

This invocation is used when nine knots are tied.

The magic began with a single knot.

My spell is done by the knot of two.

As a knot with three points, so must it be.

I keep my strength in a knot with four points.

Magic is still strong through the knot of five.

By making a knot of six, I can keep this spell safe.

A knot of seven breaks this spell.

By the knot of eight, it's all set.

By the knot of nine, I get what I want!

Hawthorn is one of the few trees that can't be cut down without causing a lot of damage in Celtic myths. Fairy music isn't something you're very good at, so look for a branch that has fallen or wood from another kind.

Chapter 5

Protection Objects and Idols

People and objects both have a certain amount of energy. This section contains lists and information on plants, stones, symbols, and other items that may be used in protective spells. These aren't the only things there are to them. They are instances that are both frequent and beneficial for self-protection. It's important researching and reading more to learn more about this topic so you can strengthen your protection magic. This will assist you in doing it better. Are you casting magic to keep your money safe? Look for plants and stones associated with money or wealth and combine them with the stones and herbs you currently use for protection.

The spells in this book may inspire you to create your own. This book has a wealth of information to assist you in this regard. Power Spellcraft for Life, a book I published, has a lot more information on how to create your own spells.

The Protection Related Colors

Adding color to your life may make it safer. People respond to color in a variety of ways. This is critical to understand before you begin. Before you employ a color in a spell, consider how you feel about it. For example, if you have negative childhood recollections of the color red, don't utilize it in spell work to make you feel secure and peaceful. Spend some time thinking about colors and writing down how they make you feel. When it comes to protection, for example, you could discover that yellow is the color that speaks to you the most.

CONSIDER YOUR LINKS

Always include your personal ties in your shopping list. Following an existing spell is a terrible idea if you don't like the materials or know that some of them don't work well for you. There's no use in devoting energy and effort since there isn't one. You may either seek for a replacement or another spell.

Here is a list of colors that are often used to protect or defend:

Black: Absorbs negative energy, repels evil, and removes negative energy.

White is a fantastic color to utilize since it cleans, calms, and signifies completeness and fresh beginnings.

blue: cleanses, eliminates negativity, and promotes honesty and communication

Red: Power, energy, halting or removing something

Gold symbolizes vitality, prosperity, good health, and happiness.

Other colors that might aid you with spell work in some of the topics covered in this book include:

Yellow-clad individuals are upbeat and pleasant. They speak effectively, travel safely, and live in a happy household.

Green represents healing, tranquility, property, belongings, and money.

Brown: transformation, soil, and property

Orange represents abundance, work, acceptance, self-esteem, motivation, and other things.

ADDING COLOR TO YOUR SPELLWORK

How can you include additional color-related energy into your spell work if you don't want to utilize candles in the colors we discussed? There are several options! Here are some suggestions:

If you wish to write spells or other things with colored pepencilspens, or markers, go ahead and do so!

Your work area should be covered with a colored cloth.

• Dress in clothing or jeweler that matches the color of the spell you're working on.

Use colored thread or cord in spells that ask for it.

• If a spell calls for a jar or bottle, use a colored one.

TO KEEP YOU SAFE, USE CRYSTALS, STONES, AND GEMS.

Many of these stones are used in the spells in this book. Here's a list of the most widely used stones in protective magic, as well as instructions on how to prepare and utilize them.

You may get started with a basic set of stones. Unless they're part of a long-term project or a charm bag, you don't always need to throw away or write off the stones you use in spells. Most of the time, they're employed to enhance an empowering or charged procedure. After that, they may be reused. This book discusses how to clean stones. Put them back in your stone box or bag so they may be used in spells again.

The Most Often Used Stones in Protective Magic

AMETHYST

Amethyst is the name given to purple quartz. It is capable of bringing the truth to light, safeguarding the body and mind, and getting things done. It is claimed to prevent you from becoming inebriated or too aroused, allowing you to keep your brain clear. It can defend against a surprise assault, treachery, and inclement weather.

Individuals who are black tourmaline

Excellent for shielding oneself from negative energy and boosting self-confidence and strength in challenging circumstances. It may assist you in determining who is to blame or who is generating problems, and it can shield you from individuals who are constantly draining your energy. Black tourmaline may be used to not only reflect or deflect bad energy, but also to transform it into good energy that can be used to aid you. It may be used to center oneself, purify your body, and ease tension, among other things.

CLEAR QUARTZ

Because it can be utilized in so many various ways, clear quartz is one of the greatest stones to employ in protective magic. It is very effective in protecting the body, mind, heart, and soul from harm. This stone is popular among new-age folks because it may function as a battery and give an alternative source of energy. Quartz is delighted to lend you its energy, and there's enough of it to go around. Clear quartz is suitable for all types of spells. You may also charge it to eliminate bad energy if you desire. Quartz is relatively simple to configure or charge for a certain purpose.

HEMATITE

It's a silver-toned stone with a hazy appearance. As a result, it, like a mirror, is effective in reflecting energy back into the air. Hematite may be utilized to keep negative energy at bay. Hematite may assist individuals who are bewildered or worried get their thinking back in order. It increases bravery, confidence, optimism, and focus.

MALACHITE

Malachite is associated with the natural world. It's wonderful if you're in an atmosphere that's giving you unpleasant feelings. It has the ability to transform negative energy into positive energy. It can filter out pollution, noise, and other environmental irritants. It is also utilized to keep individuals healthy and mend, as well as to maintain equilibrium. It is useful for safeguarding those who deal with the environment or go on travels.

OBSIDIAN

Black obsidian is useful after a shock or trauma to safeguard delicate energy and defend against any more negative events that may occur while you are attempting to recover. It is an essential stone for warding off negative energy. It may shield you from grief, bullying, and deception (such as gas lighting and ignoring), and it can help you keep negative ideas in check. It may also help individuals gain confidence and self-esteem in this manner.

Snowflake obsidian is very effective in shielding you from your own bad ideas and encouraging you to change. It is a stone that aids with concentration and grounding. It may be used to defend against mental, emotional, and physical assaults. It assists individuals and environments in releasing negative emotions and freeing up energy.

JASPER

Jasper comes in a variety of colors, the majority of which enhance bravery and guard against danger. It is often used as a worry stone to keep you calm and stable. Red jasper is associated with justice, strength, stability, endurance, and protection from physical assaults. Brown jasper is a sort of stone that is helpful for safeguarding your energy and keeping you safe in difficult circumstances for a long period.

ROSE QUARTZ

The greatest stone for making you happy. Rose quartz may help you attract and maintain good energy while dispelling bad energy. It's also a lovely stone. People utilize it for love, self-esteem, self-trust, and comfort. Rose quartz may be used in a group situation to help everyone create closer ties. You may use it to assist children and friends, as well as adults who have been emotionally or psychologically harmed. It may help defend against false rumor.

SMOKY QUARTZ

Smoky quartz absorbs bad energy and shields you from negative ideas. It also alleviates tension and panic attacks, which is beneficial when confronted with a new or risky environment. It is highly effective in grounding you and assisting you in regaining your attention and concentration. Smoky quartz, like other quartzes, may aid in the removal of negative energy. To keep intruders out of the home or automobile, and to keep the driver safe on the road. It may be used in the workplace to discourage employees from being cruel and to safeguard against bullying.

TIGER'S EYE

Tiger's eye is regarded to be a powerful, sturdy, and centering stone. It shields you from physical damage and ill luck while also encouraging you to be powerful and confident. It is beneficial to utilize it as a defense against other people's negative beliefs.

Creating and Cleaning Stones

Stones are important in spell work because they may be washed, purified and reused. There is a means for them to get rid of whatever prior energy they may have had, as well as any stray energy they may have picked up along the road. (Don't worry; it doesn't deplete their vitality.) The stone may then be used as a blank slate again.

There are several methods for cleaning a stone.

SALT

Stones may be cleaned by burying them for at least a day in a small dish of salt. If you believe the stone has a lot of junky energy or has been programmed, you may keep it there for a longer period of time.

Examine the quantity of metal in it.

Caution: Salt may corrode stones with a high iron content, so check beforehand. Also, if the stone is in a metal setting, avoid using salt to clean it. The metal may be harmed by salt.

It makes no difference what sort of salt you have. However, the more costly salt may be preferable for true spell work.

EARTH

Place the stone in an earthenware dish for three or more days. It's acceptable as long as the soil comes from your garden. Make a toothpick mark the location so you can discover the stone when the time comes. You could do this with a houseplant. If the stone contains a lot of negative energy, you should utilize a different approach. The soil will absorb that energy, which is why you should clean the stone with it. The energy will subsequently be transferred from the soil to the houseplant.

WATER

Pour some bottled spring water into a dish, place the stone in it, and then store the dish. Water is an excellent cleaning agent. The more salt you add, the more potent it becomes. Then, if there is any metal on or within the stone, use water instead of salt.

SUNLIGHT AND MOONLIGHT

The simplest approach to clean your stone is to place it on a windowsill where it will be exposed to sunlight or moonlight. Determine how long you should leave it depending on how dirty you believe the stone is. You may improve the appearance of the stone by placing it in front of a mirror.

Gods and Saints, As Well As Angels

Spell work may be used by people of any faith since it is not bound to a religion, therefore anybody can use it. However, the use of spiritual entities in spells has a long history. This was not done in this book since these spells may be utilized by individuals of any faith. If you desire, gods, saints, and angels may assist you with your spells. Include a phrase like "In the name of [religious figure], let it be so."

The list of folks above is by no means exhaustive, but it offers you a sense of the kind of people you should search for to assist you with your spells. However, calling on creatures you don't know is not a good idea. Before relying on a figure, do some reading and investigation.

CHRISTIAN FIGURES

In magic, you may seek assistance from these Christian figures.

• Archangel Michael: This angel is associated with the South and the element of fire. He is frequently shown in armor, wielding a sword or a scepter. He is a warrior associated with justice, loyalty, and defense.

• Saint Christopher: He is associated with good fortune and travel.

When people feel lonely, they remember Saint Rita. She is the patron saint of those who have been mistreated, have had disastrous marriages, or have lost their employment.

THERE IS A GOD AND A GODDESS

Many deities were approached for assistance in their respective domains. This brief list includes a few deities from many civilizations who were regarded to be adept at safeguarding and guarding humans.

• Athena: (Greek) War fought in defense, knowledge, and strategy.

• Bellona: (Roman) defense, conflict, and triumph

Tyr is a Norse word that means:

• Lakshmi: (Hindu) Fortune and deliverance from adversity.

• Vishnu: (Hindu) Protection, preservation, and order, among other things.

• Isis: (Egyptian) The healer and protector of women and children.

He is an Egyptian deity of protection and assistance.

• Green Tara: (Buddhist) Peace, protection, and a means of deflecting negative energy.

When looking for deities to utilize in protective spell work, search for those associated with war and peace, good fortune, good health or healing, and harmony. People who deal with protective spells should hunt out deities that specialize in this area. For example, if you wish to use spell work to safeguard your money, seek for deities associated with money.

ANIMALS

People in various cultures harness the energy or power of powerful animals to help them attain what they desire. You may enlist the assistance of these creatures in your spell work. They are all associated with defense and protection; thus, they may assist you.

Also, consider what you want to do.

If you already appreciate an animal, ask it for assistance, even if it doesn't seem to be guarding you. That animal means a lot to you, and that may be enough.

• Lion: Courage, patience, power, and strength; also, a protector character in many different civilizations.

Bravery, Strength, Power, Fortune, and Change

A bird of prey must confront many challenges that need bravery, resilience, clarity, knowledge, and strength.

Wolf like things like pack, caring for others, teaching, freedom, and intuition.

Herbs are utilized to keep people safe

Herbs are an excellent approach to enhance your defense by interacting with natural energy. They're compact, adaptable, and a lot of fun to use.

You probably already have a lot of spices in your spice cupboard. These include herbs such as bay and sage, as well as spices such as salt. Outside, you may find nettle, cedar, and juniper. Although angelica and rue are difficult to locate, they may both be cultivated at the same time. Other plants may need to be purchased from an herb store or online.

Unless otherwise specified, herbs are usually used dry. Herbs are sometimes dried for spells, but if they're still fresh, lay them out on a parchment-lined baking sheet and bake them at low heat (no more than 175°F) for 90 minutes to 4 hours, depending on how wet they are. The herbs will be entirely dried this way.

Check on the herbs in the oven every 15 minutes or so to make sure they're still warm. Allow the oven door to remain open for approximately one hour. Remove the baking sheet from the oven and set it aside to cool until the leaves can be crumbled between your fingers. Herb sprigs that are light or little will dry faster than sprigs that are bulky.

Once dried, you may preserve them whole or crush the leaves and store them in spice jars.

Separate your herbs!

Is it logical to keep your magical herbs separate from the ones you use to produce food? That is all up to you. This isn't always the case. Go ahead and do it as long as you're comfortable getting some rosemary from the spice jar in the pantry. You're going to have to clean it regardless. If you don't want to, that's great, too. Keep a second set of herbs with your other tools while you're casting spells.

You may defend yourself by using the following basic herbs:

Angelica is the individual in this case (ANGELICA ARCHANGELICA)

Angelica has a great deal of defensive energy. It may be used to fend off illness, bad luck, and evil, as well as to safeguard a house. It also makes you more courageous, particularly if you're in a morally decent position. Angelica is a potent amulet in and of itself. Its protecting aura extends to the home and the area surrounding it when it grows in a garden.

The Bay Leaf (LAURUS NOBILIS)

The bay laurel's leafy portions are very effective in protecting you, making you wiser, removing bad luck, and making money. There are several additional uses for Bay, such as protecting your health and celebrating triumph.

CEDAR is a dog's name (CEDRUS SPP.)

Cedar is incredibly effective at removing negative energy while leaving a lot of positive energy behind. It may assist to defend against negative energy, repel evil, promote optimism and compassion, and aid in healing. Wet and chopped cedar fronds or crushed cedar bark may be employed.

Search from corn (CINNAMOMUM VERUM, CINNAMOMUM CASSIA)

This spice is beneficial to your health and well-being, as well as your vitality, money, healing, and love! Sprinkle cinnamon on a spell that needs a boost of power.

Take care of one another (SYZYGIUM AROMATICUM)

Cloves are very effective in dispelling rumors, putting an end to gossip, and protecting your reputation from false allegations, making them extremely beneficial. They offer good fortune, wealth, and excellent money transactions, as well as healing energies. They do the following:

Garlic is a kind of vegetable (ALLIUM SATIVUM)

Garlic is utilized to promote courage, develop determination, defend against evil, and improve and protect health. Garlic may also help and safeguard your health. You may take your energy with you at all times to keep it secure. Garlic braids strung about the home helps dispel negative energy and luck. Garlic may be used fresh or dried, and it can be prepared in a variety of ways.

Juniper's given name is (JUNIPERUS COMMUNIS)

Juniper has considerable power to defend you. It may guard against theft and accidents. Juniper is also used to bring good luck, keep people healthy, decrease anxiety, increase attention and clarity, and clean things up. Juniper may be utilized in the form of ground wood or shaved wood. It's also good for making berries.

Lemons are a kind of fruit (CITRUS LIMON)

Lemon, which is purifying and astringent, may also be utilized in simple rituals for happiness and communication. It is useful for clearing out muddy or sluggish energy and for shutting off bad energy. Depending on the spell, fresh lemons, lemon juice, or dried lemon zest might be utilized.

The word nettle refers to a plant that grows in the (URTICA DIOICA)

Snails are excellent for defensive magic, particularly when combined with spells that return energy to its source. They are also utilized for healing, bravery, and staying out of trouble, and they are quite significant. To prevent getting nettles in your eyes, handle fresh nettles with gloves. The herb is often dried and minced, although it may also be used fresh.

It's an onion (ALLIUM CEPA)

Onions are utilized to defend and exorcise, as well as to ward off illness and evil spirits. Onions are often employed in defensive magic because they can absorb bad energy.

Rosemarie's given name is Rosemarie (ROSMARINUS OFFICINALIS)

Rosemary is beneficial for safeguarding you, removing negative energy, and boosting your memory. Use rosemary to think optimistically, which is beneficial for any kind of spell work! This herb improves confidence and helps to eliminate negative ideas.

Resume (RUTA GRAVEOLENS)

Rue, the grace plant, has a long history of being used to protect, expel, and fend off evil. Sprigs of it may be used to sprinkle Blessed Water or other infusions over persons and locations, a practice known as "asperging." People used to hang sprigs of rue over doorways and windows to ward off illness, bad luck, and negative energy.

Sage: This is what Sage has to say (SALVIA SPP.)

Sage is quite skilled at getting rid of things that aren't beneficial for her. The classic smudge stick is comprised of sage or a mixture of sage and other cleansing herbs. Growing sage is thought to make individuals live longer lives, making it an excellent plant to utilize in spells that assist in healing or improving one's health. Sage is a soothing plant that is also associated with money, knowledge, and business. In reality, the word salvia implies "to guard, save, or heal."

Sage can be used with any type of plant. The most popular kind is culinary sage, Salvia officialism, which can be found in most supermarkets' spice aisles. White sage (Salvia ananas), blue sage (Salvia Clevelander), purple sage (Salvia ludophile), and black sage (Salvia ananas) may also be found in esoteric stores (Salvia mellifera). Some herbs are referred to be sage, although not all of them are. To be sure, double-check the Latin name.

Salt

The greatest thing you can do to protect yourself is to use salt. Although salt is a mineral, it is commonly regarded of as a herb since it is a food, is easy to get, and is simple to use.

Salt absorbs and retains negative energy. By sprinkling it into a bath, it can help you get rid of negative energy that has become attached to your body. It may be used to eliminate negative energy from objects by placing them in a salt bowl or plate. A dish of salt may be placed in a room to clear off unwanted energies. After using salt to clean or purify, it should not be used again. You may get rid of it by carefully pouring it down the sink while running the water.

Black salt was traditionally created by combining normal salt with iron. This variety of black salt is still available for purchase. To manufacture it, combine fire ashes with it. "Hawaiian black salt" is made by combining coconut-shell charcoal powder with Hawaiian sea salt. It's food-grade salt, so it's completely safe to use. You may also use pink Himalayan salt, although normal salt will be enough for this dish.

For roads, there is just ROAD SALT

Use no road salt. It is the natural, unprocessed salt that comes from the earth. It is often used with anti-cling compounds or other chemicals that aid in the melting of ice. In the winter, you should not use it to avoid people from slipping and falling on your driveway, walkway, and stairs.

Where Should Herbs Be Placed and How Should They Be Used?

Herbs, like stones, should be cleaned before being used. When it comes to gathering energy, though, not all stones function the same way. You may perform the following before using herbs:

1. The center and ground.

2. Place your hands on top of the herb. This is the next phase.

3. Draw energy from the ground and bring it to the surface. Allow the water to trickle down your arms to your hands and the herb as you move your arms.

4. Say aloud, "With this energy, you are cleansed, free of everything that is not yours."

5. The herb is usable.

After cleaning the herb, it may be preserved. Before using the herb again, check its energy to determine whether it has to be cleansed again. If you're unsure what to do, just do it. It's fast and won't do any harm.

Many plants have been used in spells to enhance energy, either by dispersing them about a specified spot or by including them in a charm bag. However, there are alternative applications for them.

Decoctions and infusions

You're preparing a tea mix the next time you prepare tea. To infuse, place a plant in hot water for a brief period of time to extract its qualities. Decoction: A drink is made by boiling an herb in water. Using either approach, you may create a liquid that can be used for a number of purposes, such as wiping off objects, walls, or floors, anointing the body or hair, or spraying in a spray bottle. It may be stored in the fridge for a few days in a tightly sealed jar or container.

Oils that have been infected with herbs

Herbs are made into oils by combining them with oils such as olive or sunflower. Fill a clean container halfway with chopped dry herbs to make herb-infused oil. Then, gradually pour in enough oil to cover the herbs and shake the container. It's critical that the oil gets to all of the herbal matter. Then screw the lid on the jar and give it a gentle shake.

To keep the jar cold, shake it every few days. After three weeks, begin testing to see whether the oil has soaked in enough to allow you to utilize it. Leave it for up to 6 weeks with dense, thick plants; the additional time will allow the oil to extract the herbal essence from them.

To strain the oil into clean storage bottles, use cheesecloth or another filter. Squeeze any herb-soaked oil that has been steeped in it to extract as much as possible. The storage bottles should be labeled and the lids secured. It must be used within a year. These oils can be used to draw protective symbols on walls, doors, and other surfaces. They may also be used to anoint the body or added to bath water. Cinnamon may be harmful to your skin, so use with caution.

Incense

Incense in the shape of a stick or cone is the most frequent. It's made of powdered wood that's been shaped (around a thin wooden center, in the case of a stick). To make the sticks and cones smell pleasant, oils are drizzled over them.

You may manufacture your own incense using plants and resins. It may be burned on charcoal tablets, which are available at new age stores and religious supply stores. Dried herbs may be burned directly on the charcoal, although they have a strong odor and burn fast. You can make frankincense smell sweeter by combining dried plants with frankincense resin. This improves the scent, provides additional protecting or purifying energy, and extends the burn time. You may purchase frankincense granules at new-age and religious shops, or you can get them online. If you desire, you may also add a few drops of essential oil to your incense mix. Write down your mix so you may adjust or replicate the formula in the future. If you produce enough incense to store, mark the jar so you can locate it when you want to manufacture more.

Powders are strewn over the ground.

To prepare powders, dried herbs are crushed extremely finely, either by hand using a mortar and pestle or in an herb-only coffee grinder. Unless you want coffee powder in your herbs and coffee powder in your herbs! You may use them as a stand-alone ingredient or combine them with other herbs before or after powdering.

Sprinkle powders may be used to assist in the cleaning of areas. Spritz them on the floor, let them sit for a few minutes, then sweep them up and toss them outdoors. Pinches of herb powder can be used in spells that call for dried herbs, sprinkled on your doorstep, or used to protect your home and possessions outside. Use herb powder to produce body powder, dust linens on the bed, or clean the carpet by combining it with rice flour or cornstarch.

Potpourri

Potpourri is a simple mixture of dry herbs in a bowl or jar, occasionally with the addition of a drop or two of essential oil. There are several plants that may be utilized for magic or to make one smell nice. It's possible that dried rose petals, sandalwood chips, and dried carnation petals smell nice together. You might also add a pinch of cinnamon, rosemary, and a few bay leaves to the concoction to further protect yourself.

Chapter 6

Full Moon Spell

It's true. The full moon is a rare time when great energy vibrations are released, and many people strive to harness this magical force via specialized rituals. Protecting your relationship, removing yourself from a detrimental influence, breaking a bad habit... There are rituals for all of our wishes and requirements. They help us infuse our goals and act with enhanced vitality when used on a full moon night... Today, we've decided to provide you with four rituals centered on cleaning and safeguarding your house.

Full moon ritual n°1: Sage cleaning of areas

The full moon's energy is incredibly cleansing, and when utilized appropriately, it may help us get rid of the bad vibes and negative energies that gather around us. To achieve this, just burn a stick of sage in an abalone shell (or any fireproof container!), then disseminate the smoke over the space you want to clear. If you like, you may spread the smoke with a feather, which will also enable you to summon the angels to your side and send pleasant waves to the procedure. At the conclusion of the ceremony, open all the windows to allow the smoke to evaporate and bring in new, fresh energy.

Sage should be avoided by pregnant and nursing women due to its abortive effects, as well as persons suffering from epilepsy.

Full moon ceremony n°2: Light recharging of stones

The full moon is the ideal moment to recharge crystals, releasing them from stagnated energy and energizing their vibrations. To do this, the stones are put outside or on a window sill and kept exposed to the moonlight for the whole night. However, in the event of rain, protect those who cannot endure water and retrieve those who should not be exposed to direct sunlight in the early morning.

Before recharging, it is critical to cleanse your stones (with pure water, salt, burying, etc.) to remove any stored sluggish energy.

Full moon ritual n°3: Using salt to chase evil waves

To keep unwanted influences and negative energies out of your house, sprinkle salt in front of your home's entrances as a protective barrier (doors, windows, gates, etc.). Run a small trickle of salt over the whole width of the aperture, with the distinct aim of purifying your house and blocking the access to bad energy. Allow it to dry overnight or for a few days before sweeping, picking up, and burning. The harmful waves will have been absorbed by the salt, and by burning them, you will keep them away from your house.

Full moon ritual n°4: Symbolic protection for your house

The pentacle, triskelion, and pentagram are the most potent protective symbols. To safeguard a room or an item, create the sign of your choice with your finger or the flame of a candle on a piece of paper, on a wall, or even fictitiously in the air, linking it with a defensive purpose.

Be cautious; these rituals are easy and need minimal resources, but they must be performed with sincerity. It's similar to reciting a prayer. To gain results, you must believe in it, therefore don't forget to accompany each of these routines with good thoughts and confidence.

It is here and ready for you to release you from the regular nocturnal tumults and help you get a decent night's sleep. Yoga Nidra, meditation, breathing and visualization techniques are on the agenda... The entire package to relax your body and mind at night and turn your restless nights into dreamy evenings!

Spell for Healing, and Purification Spells

As the new year approaches, our natural impulse is to set plans, objectives, and promises of progress. Aside from a list of commitments (which may be impacted by a range of events), it is vital to thank the previous year and prepare ourselves in every way for a symbolic new beginning.

The following spells are ideal for any occasion, but they work particularly well to start off the new year.

Gratitude and Blessings Spell

End and start the year by noting your advantages and building the discipline of thanks.

You will need a handful of 50 or more relatively tiny objects that you appreciate for this exercise. Pebbles, seashells, or even beans may be utilized. Ideally, choose something that will last the full year.

Light your preferred candles and maybe some essential smells that provide you comfort. Place your items in front of you on the floor, surrounded by candles. Each item indicates a benefit in your life for which you are appreciative or hope to manifest in the next year.

Take the first object that represents a blessing you obtained this year and express your thanks openly (for example, "thank you for my employment," "thank you for my family's health"). Continue in this way with everything you obtain. Once you've completed the list, see another handful of your possessions encircled by light.

Consider that all items are encircled and energized by the creative light. One by one, repeat the Spell, expressing thanks for the blessings you want to receive in the new year (for example, "thank you for my new work," "thank you for my recovered health").

After that, focus on the objects and envision them vibrating with white light while stating aloud, "This or something better emerges in my life in the most beneficial way for everyone concerned."

Place your "blessings" in a prominent location where they will be seen throughout the year.

Forgiveness and letting go have a magical effect.

The most effective strategy for moving ahead in life and attracting more blessings is to release what no longer serves us and keeps us trapped. This is a potent Forgiveness Spell that we may use on others or on ourselves.

Allow yourself ten minutes alone to sit comfortably, focus on your breathing, and meditate. Make a mental note of the items you desire to discard. Consider it thoroughly, experience it, and live it to the hilt (if you feel ready for it). Consider the situation or person in front of you and see a bright pink light in your chest and a bright purple light in the center of your forehead.

Propel these two lights toward the situation or person in front of you (as if they were a line linking your body to them) and watch as a giant balloon develops around that situation. In-depth examination of the pink and purple light balloon that encircles the scene or person. It is a robust balloon.

Experiment: attempt to rupture the balloon with a huge needle, but it will not work.

Consider the scenario as being surrounded by pink and purple lights and enclosed for a few seconds by the powerful balloon. Give thanks for everything you've learned and bless the experience, regardless of how painful it was.

When you're ready, take a step back and watch the balloon begin to rise, gliding through the air into the sky. Notice how the rope of light flowing from his body keeps him from soaring over a certain point? Now see a giant pair of scissors encircled by white light, and cut the connection connecting it to the globe. Observe the balloon as it ascends to an almost invisible point and then goes forever into the sky.

Feel glad that you will never have to deal with this situation again, since your emotional reaction to it has ceased to exist.

Cleansing Spell Using Salt Water

Utilizing sea salt in a simple but effective Spell to cleanse a location and its aura is a wonderful way to do this.

Purchase fine sea salt and dilute one cup in four glasses of warm water to create space. Shake your hand as you go around your house in order, from the front entryway to the final room, or vice versa. Spray the ceilings, corners, behind furniture, and in the center of the room, seeing white light beams originating from your hand and covering all surfaces. Declare aloud your favorite affirmation (one that expresses your intention) or this one: "Only divine light, love, peace, and fortune enter and remain in our home, guarding and protecting us at all times." Consider the possibility that this is already a reality. (Keep in mind that salt water may discolor your furniture temporarily.)

To balance and cleanse your aura, take a bath or shower with fine sea salt. Beginning at your feet, continue massaging this salt in circles around your skin, working your way up to your head, handful by handful. Make certain that no part of your body is left unclothed. Increase your time spent going through the chakras. You'll immediately notice a difference. Recite your preferred affirmation while visualizing a warm bath of energy enveloping you on all sides. Consider white light emanating from the crown of your head and exploding into a rainbow of colors that shower down on you until you reach your head (don't forget to lightly touch your face). Consider for a minute seeing and feeling your body vibrating with a new life-giving energy that will only attract the good and heavenly while guarding you from the undesirable. Once completed, rinse well with warm and then cold water. Sensitize yourself to safety, health, and tranquility.

Spells using incense for the home and business

Incense sticks are used in a variety of Spells, some of which are utilized in religious ceremonies. The primary goal of this practice is to cleanse the surrounding area's energy via the use of herbs or incense. The goal is to use plants that are capable of transmuting negative energies into positive ones, thereby purifying the body and space of any energy parasite. Two of the most often used incense sticks are sage and sandalwood. Incense does not have to be elaborate; for instance, a single incense stick may serve.

To empty a place, work in a circular motion from the room's periphery to its center, as though in a spiral. Contrary to popular belief, the counterclockwise direction is often employed to diminish or reject, while the clockwise direction is frequently used to promote, increase, and strengthen. Don't forget to check the space's corners, as well as behind and behind large pieces of furniture, since these are common areas for energy to gather.

Intention and focus are critical components of any energy practice. Ascertain that you will not be interrupted, and utilize quiet or spiel music to provide a serene and soothing atmosphere. Determine the purpose of the Spell and compose one or two affirmations.

Repeat your affirmations calmly and confidently as you move the incense throughout your house, imagining the reality you intend to create. She may rest at the completion of the Spell, knowing that the space has been cleansed and his objective has started to manifest.

Spell of Rapid Protection

This vision is beneficial for safeguarding your vehicle, home, family, or yourself and will immediately bring you tranquility.

Begin by imagining the top half of a sphere of light descending from the heavens and resting like a strong shield over your head. Consider the lower half of the same ball of light, radiating with the ferocity of fire from the earth's core and softly climbing to rest under your feet. Consider cords of light coming into your brain from the top half sphere and roots of light dropping into your feet from the bottom half sphere at the same time.

Sensitize yourself to the power of the universe and the earth coursing through your body, converging in the center of your chest, and spiraling into a great flash of light. Sensitize yourself as this spiral of light increases and wraps around your whole body, connecting the spheres and producing a solid barrier. Consider the outside of this shield as a mirror that allows only light to flow through while reflecting the dark and negative.

Rep the imagery, this time with your family, your home, or any other object or person you want to shield with this shield of light.

Cleansing and protection bath

Additionally, this Spell is recommended at times of physiological pain or sickness.

Begin with an imagery of a shower. Watch as the water transforms into light and penetrates your body, softly cleansing it from the inside out.

Consider how everything that is no longer beneficial to you (pain, wrath, resentment) begins to condense and concentrate in the center of your chest, forming an oil-like fluid. When everything is collected in the chest, observe how the water/light arrives in the same spot and begins to push the darkness towards your feet, eventually replacing it. Where once there was darkness, there is now tranquility and brightness. (If you're using this Spell to alleviate pain or defeat a disease, see the region in issue as black and viscous, then transforming into a soothing, relaxing light.)

Sensitize yourself to the gentle drip of this viscous fluid till it emerges from your foot and enters the earth. (If you are within a structure, track the oil down each level until it reaches and penetrates the dirt.) Follow it as it journeys to the earth's core, which is brimming with light, fire, life, and power, and see how the dark and viscous substance merges with the light until it is entirely rejuvenated.

Rest assured that every darkness has been transformed into light and power, enabling the planet to continue producing life. Everything in his body is made of light, which provides him with nourishment and protection.

Love Spell

A ritual is a powerful approach to concentrate on a request in order to make it come true. In this situation, the goal is love (or interest or attraction - you decide). If you believe in love and the power of sending powerful, good thoughts to the world to receive what you desire, continue reading to discover how to cast a spell that will bring you the love you want.

Make use of a ready-made spell

A straightforward love spells. This is a simple magic that does not need any fancy materials or astrological charts. If you're seeking for more than just a buddy, this spell will help you attract more of them while also enhancing your sexuality. If you have a specific individual in mind, concentrate on them throughout this ritual to attract them or enhance the link that already exists.

• **Thoroughly clean the bathroom.** We're not talking about spiritual cleansing here; we're talking about deep cleaning with detergents and antibacterial. Towels or sheets in white or pink should be used to cover the mirrors.

• **Fill the tub with water and toss in a handful of sea salt, stating, "Negativity has been washed away.** I'm a new person as of today! Many people's heads will turn as I pass, including those I choose to remain with."

• **Place three white votive candles or three floating candles in the tub.** As you prepare to enter the water, relax and concentrate on your body, thinking about how sensuous and beautiful you are. Concentrate on what you like about yourself. If you're performing this spell on someone in particular, start concentrating on them right now.

• **If possible, turn off the light and listen to your favorite music.** Choose music that corresponds to your final purpose.

• **If you want wild and passionate love, search for anything that makes you feel unconstrained and seductive.** If you're seeking for a soul mate and someone who will make you feel secure, listen to music that will make you feel tranquil and at ease. What you need for a widespread attraction is a pleasant and lovely tune.

• **Soak in the tub and unwind.** At least once, make sure that every portion of your body is totally immersed in water. Shave your head if required. Cleaning is an important aspect of the ritual.

• **Once finished, say the words of the spell you uttered before entering the tub.** Add the following statement to the conclusion of the spell this time: "I am blessed, I am loving, I am adored, and I am self-loving. I am in love!"

• **Trust your instincts and add additional things if you believe it is the best option for you.** Light an incense stick, add herbal bath oils or essential oils, your favorite scent, a cup of herbal tea, or a sponge purchased specifically for this ritual.

Lost Love's Spell

If you had love but lost it due to circumstances, personal challenges, or outside interference, you may perform this spell to attempt to reclaim it.

• **Purchase six candles.** Each hue will need a candle: red, green, yellow, and blue. Two pink candles are also required.

• **Arrange candles in the four cardinal directions.** The red candle should be placed in the southernmost corner of your area, the green candle in the northernmost corner, the yellow candle in the east, and the blue candle in the westernmost corner.

• **Extinguish the six candles.** Hold the pinks in your hands and face the red candle. Recite the following line until you're satisfied: "Hear my petition, glorious Goddess and great God! Burn my desire three times, Lord of Fire. Bring (insert name) back to me if it is fate."

Spell of Soul Mate. This spell is intended to attract the ideal spouse for you at this time in your life. But, before you perform this magic, be sure you're prepared for this level of devotion. If you're only looking to find who's "right" for you, don't do the ritual. You must be willing to accept responsibility for every event and consequence.

• **Before beginning this spell, you will need to do some preparation.** Collect meaningful paper for yourself, such as parchment, cotton or hemp paper, or a piece of patterned paper. You will also need a ritual writing instrument. You may use a goose feather, a fountain pen, your favorite ballpoint pen, or a fine-tipped marker once again. It doesn't have to be something you use on a daily basis to make your shopping list. Finally, retrieve the moon incense and charcoal, as well as a heart-shaped or heart-decorated box.

• **Choose the best moment.** This spell should be performed at night, preferably during the growing moon. With the power of moon incense at your disposal, you will be able to be flexible with the schedule without jeopardizing the outcomes.

• **Fortify your aura by meditating and/or cleaning.** Write words of power that will conjure up the ideal match for you right now, using the paper and pen for the ceremony. Don't mention specific names or ponder about a specific individual. You may or may not have found your soul partner, so keep all options open.

• **If you can't think of anything else, try these: "This magic will call my soul mate tonight if she exists.** My soul partner will find a way to get in touch with me. I create this request out of pure love and complete faith, not desire. This magic will assist us in coming together, but free will not fail us tonight."

• **When you're finished, review what you've written to ensure that you've conveyed all you meant to say and**

haven't left anything out. After that, meditate by starting your ceremonial fire on coal.

• **Keep meditating until you feel that everything is alright, that your will is solid, and you have a feeling of assurance.** Read what you've written three times when the fire is nearly out and the coal is blazing. Sprinkle roughly a spoonful of moon incense over the fire while you read or at the conclusion of each iteration.

• **It's ideal to practice using moon incense with a ceremonial fire if you've never done so before.** Because the flames will engulf the trail of incense powder, you must proceed with caution. It will also produce sparks, which are as harmful. Throw the incense all at once, without leaving trails or sprinkling it. Wearing too-loose clothes with long sleeves is not recommended. Take extreme caution.

• **Fold the paper and put it in the heart box to serve as your spell box.** Place it in a secure location with favorable vibes. Forget about it now. Allow nature, destiny, and spirits to work together to bring your soul partners to you.

Create your Own Personalized Love Spell

1. Set a goal for yourself. Do you want someone to take notice of you? Do you want to be attracted to a mysterious stranger? How can you get rid of the negative energy from a poor relationship? Want to spice up your love life? How can you make your interactions with the universe more loving? The most crucial component is visualization; therefore, you must have a very clear image of what you want to accomplish in mind.

• Consider the possible negative consequences of your aim. For example, if you wish to attract your soul mate, consider if you are at the ideal point in your life to get into such a relationship. If you wish to cast a spell on someone you don't know well, keep in mind that this individual may not be all that intriguing when seen up close.

• Keep the rule of three in mind. Rede Wicca claims that "Everything you do has a three-fold positive and three-fold negative repercussion. If you do good, you will be rewarded three times; if you do evil, you will be rewarded three times." Attract love by freely sharing affection.

• Stay away from intents that entail power, manipulation, or otherwise manipulating the other person. These intentions position you to get the same thing in return. For example, instead of attracting someone who is overly possessive and extremely jealous of you, you may be attracting someone who is overly possessive and extremely jealous of you.

2. Obtain symbolically appropriate material. What you pick and the combinations you make will serve as the foundation for the kind of love you want to attract.

• Begin with the colors. Red, for example, is a hue that is often linked with passion and desire. Pink is the hue of the heart, yet it draws a kinder love. White represents innocence and is appropriate for a platonic connection. Green is connected with nature and might be utilized to boost masculinity. Choose candles, clothing, paper, flowers, and other goods in a color that corresponds to your requirements.

• Include spices or herbs in the spell. Lemon balm and catnip, according to folklore, may be used to attract love, while marjoram is said to drive away negativity and encourage love and happiness. Lavender is maybe the most effective plant for seducing guys. If your request is more sexual in nature, try vervain, which the Druids used to enhance love, desire, and sexual fulfillment, cumin, which stimulates lust and faithfulness, or cinnamon and fennel to boost vitality and libido.

• Employ symbolic things. Conduct some research on symbols associated with common things. You're likely to discover many interpretations for the same object, so trust your instincts and choose one that speaks to you.

• Use a mirror to get a good look at yourself, silk for sensuality, flowers for romance, lingerie for libido, or anything else that has particular importance for you.

• If your spell is intended at a specific individual and you have anything that belongs to him (hair, clothes, a letter, something you loaned him), remember to include it in the ritual.

• Avoid using things with negative connotations, such as needles, knives, ropes, or other objects with violent connotations; this might give your ceremony an unpleasant twist.

3. Cleanse the body. Use herbs, flowers, or essential oils to create a ceremonial bath. Infuse the water with roses, jasmine, or one of the herbs listed above. Take a bath by candlelight if feasible. Put on clean clothing after you're finished. Put on new clothing if you've picked one for the ceremony.

4. Select a seat. Cast the magic in a quiet area where you will not be disturbed. It would be wonderful to have a romantic place accessible, such as a forest or a beach; nevertheless, your goal must be seclusion and the ability to concentrate, so remaining inside in a clean, pleasant room is good.

5. Make a circle. To protect the area, you wish to work in, make a circle of sea salt (with or without rosemary). If required, ignite a sage bouquet and distribute the smoke to rid the environment of any negativity.

6. Light the candles and concentrate. Concentrate on your aim. Visualize the event as if you were really living it; make it as real as possible by envisioning it with all of your senses.

Make your wish loudly if you desire; otherwise, repeat it in your brain or write it on a piece of paper and burn it, enabling it to escape into the cosmos.

• If you wish, do a rhyming spell. It will increase the potency of the ceremony. You might even conjure up the name of a deity or goddess who corresponds to your particular ideology. Try not to be a poet. If you can, rhyming lines is nice, but what counts is the sincerity and good intentions of your remarks.

• Make a symbolic proposal. Appropriate offerings include out, an apple, some wine, or anything of personal importance.

• Do not disrupt the candles and do not extinguish them prematurely. Allow them to wear out entirely before collecting the wax and storing it in a sack under your pillow or burying it in the garden to grow - ideally in an area where your dog would not dig.

7. Repeat to ramp up the effect. The stronger the signal you give out, the more focused you are on your objective. Perform this ceremony on a daily, weekly, or full moon basis, or as frequently as seems right, and be thankful for the development.

8. Keep an open mind to the possibilities. The outcomes may be different - or even better - than expected. Don't get so caught up in a certain picture of love that you lose out on a good chance that comes your way.

Advice

• Wear rose quartz jeweler to attract love.

• For added potency, engrave mystical symbols or your name on the candle.

• If possible, do the ceremony on a full moon night.

• Make whatever changes you desire to the ritual. You may dance, sing, or do whatever else makes you feel loved.

Warnings

• Passers-by may find your actions unusual or unpleasant.

• You can't make someone love you if he doesn't want to.

Money Spells

Some subjects are more magical and have more spells and attention than others. People are more interested in weather spells, invisibility spells, and animal preservation rituals. Love, protection, fertility, and healing spells get a more general response. Money is another universal category that is linked to each other. Everyone could use more.

if there was a spell that made people rich quickly, there would be a lot more witches, fortunetellers, and shamans who would be very rich. As we all know, and as people who don't like magic like to point out, this isn't true. People who are interested in metaphysics, from Dr. Dee to Dr. John, and from Madame Blavatsky to the Count of Cagliostro, are not wealthy.

Suggestions on how to make money

Gold and **green** are the main colors.

Because it represents the idea of doubling, **2** is the most important number.

In ancient Rome, **Mercury** was a Roman deity who was linked to money and wealth.

Jupiter, on the other hand, is a planet of good fortune.

The **Moon**, on the other hand, is a planet of magic and wishes that come true. Spells for money or business growth should be cast when the moon is getting bigger.

However, there are a few things to think about.

Every person doesn't get the same thing, but the benefits of being in the world of the mind go beyond the tangible. Some magical practitioners have lived at least for a time from hand to mouth, so there are a wide range of magical spells that can be used in any situation.

Money Spell with Alfalfa.

Over alfalfa, talk about your money dreams. If it isn't burned, the ashes should be spread around your land.

Spells of Animal Magic for Money

People who help with Animal Magic Wealth Spell

An animal called a frog is a good friend of money and wealth. A toad is also good for money and wealth. A snake is also good for money and wealth. Surround yourself with pictures of them to make money and inspire you to make money.

Chinese Animal Magic Spells for Wealth in China

Animal amulets are used in Chinese magic. These are usually small figurines of different animals sitting on a big bed of money. These amulets are used to bring good fortune and to keep what already exists safe from harm.

There is a three-legged toad that is the most well-known. It is shown sitting on a pile of money. Magical money toads have a slightly open mouth, which allows a fake Chinese coin to be inserted.

There should be no money toad on the floor. It should be kept at a coffee table height.

Put his "magic coin" in his mouth and turn him so that he is facing away from the door.

When he gets tired, take the coin out of his mouth and turn the toad so that he can rest and recharge.

When installing toads, make sure they are always facing the front door. You can use more than one toad at the same time. Rotate the toads so that there is always at least one person who can do the job.

The Chinese Frog Animal Magic Wealth Spell

Frogs are thought to be the best example of growth, reproduction, and diversity. The hieroglyph for "tadpole" was used by the ancient Egyptians to show how many they could say.

Place a money frog charm on top of real coins on a dish.

Sprinkle a mixture of Money Drawing Powder and magnetic sand over the surface of the dough.

Under your bed, facing the door.

Sprinkle with more powder as needed.

The dragon-tortoise, mongoose, and cow are some of the other wealth-making Chinese animal amulets. All of them are lying on a treasure hoard. This cow is one of the many holy cows on Earth, and if she brings you money, you must not eat meat in return. For single moms and their kids, the picture of a sow feeding her piglets on a bed of coins is said to be very helpful.

Golden Spider Animal Magic Wealth Spells for Animals

The golden money spider weaves a web of money. A long-running myth says that killing a spider is bad luck if you want to stay alive and grow.

Draw a picture of a spider hiding in its labyrinthine web on red paper with gold ink.

Second, put the picture in a corner and put a saucer under it.

Make a spell and throw a few pennies into the saucer as you do it, too. Inform the spider of your needs.

Once a week, or when the spider comes through for you, add a few more pennies to the dish.

Japanese Frog Animal Magic Spells for Wealth

According to Japanese tradition, having a small picture of a frog in your wallet increases your wealth. There are two ways to do this. Also, you could look for a small Japanese wallet frog charm that is small enough to fit in a wallet, like one that is flat enough. Charge the frog with your wishes and use your money to move it to where you want it. Alternatively, you could put a picture or sketch of a green frog inside your wallet.

An animal magic wealth spell called "Maneki Neko"

Because the Japanese beckoning cat, Maneki Neko, is so popular, she has been used for many different things. Her main job is to make money for her owner. This amulet shows a cat sitting down with one hand raised in the Japanese sign for "Come here." Requests for more business are made by Maneki Neko with his left hand raised. Requests for money are made by Maneki Neko with his right hand raised in legend, if you have a high hand, you'll have a more powerful amulet.

People say that a gold cat can help you get more money. Maneki Neko comes in a variety of colors, all of which can help you get rich.

- Maneki Neko must face the outside world in order to bring money into your secret place.
- Place Maneki Neko at a window that looks out into the outside or across from the front door. This is the second step.
- Some Maneki Neko have a hole on the back, like a child's piggy bank. Make a wish and put a few pennies in the amulet to make it work.

There is an Avocado Money Curse

Money comes to avocado trees because they look like money. Make sure to plant an avocado tree and eat the first avocado that grows from it. Before you use it as a money charm, clean and dry its hole.

Spell of Peruvian Balsam

Peruvian balsam isn't just found in Peru. It grows all over Central and South America, not just there. In addition to its religious and medicinal properties, it is also used in magic to bring money. Burning Peruvian balsam will bring you happiness and good fortune.

Botanicals for the basics of money

Botanicals that look like money and money-drawing plants are on this list. Aloe, avocado, clover and chamomile can all be used in spells. Alfalfa, avocado, basil and cabbage can also be used. Chamomile, clover and dill can also be used in spells. Lettuce and mint can also be used. Poppies and vervain can also be used in spells, as can five-finger grass (cinquefoil).

A money candle made of botanicals.

Hold a green candle in your hands and charge it with your goal. Hollow it out, fill it with money-making plants, and then burn it.

Spells made by Basil.

Basil is an herb that is often linked to money and growth. It is used to attract and boost wealth, fertility, and romance, as well as to improve fertility and romance. Indian Lakshmi and Vodou's Ezili Freda Dahomey are both very powerful Wealth Spirits, so the plant is a big deal to both of them.

Bath Basil Spell

The smell of basil on the skin is said to bring money to the person who wears it. People in Spain used to bathe in basil and rub the smell all over their bodies to get clients who were willing to spend money. Even if you don't work in the same field, you can follow the tradition. Bathe before going out to look for money. In this spell, basil smells so good.

1. Slice the majority of a big bunch of basil to get the volatile oils out. Keep some leaves whole, especially the ones that look like dollar bills.

2. Put the basil in a bowl and cover it with hot water.

3. Putting it in the bath when it's cool. It's a good idea to float the whole leaf in the water, so you can imagine swimming in cash.

4. Let the water dry off of you before you let it air-dry.

In number five, don't throw away the used basil leaves or your money. However, you can either leave them in the tub until your transactions are done, or you can take them, put them in a bag, and keep them until a good time to get rid of them comes along.

The exact sum it's Basil Spell.

If you need an exact amount of money, write it down on paper.

Add a little basil oil to the paper.

The third step is to fold it in half twice and put it in an earthenware flower pot. (Save crossroads dirt to get more bonus points.)

The best thing to do is to put money-attracting plants in the pot, like marigolds, basil, thyme, or even a strong cactus in it.

Make a money spell with Bayberry.

1. Dip a small piece of silver in oil that has been infused with bayberry.

2. Hold it in your left hand and charge it with what you want.

3. Carry it with you all day.

4. Every day, put it on your forehead above your Third Eye spot for 30 minutes. When you feed once a week, give it a little bit of bayberry oil to drink.

Putting a spell on Bryony Root

As a substitute for the rare Mediterranean plant, white bryony is also known as English or European Mandrake. This is because it is one of the most common roots to use as a substitute. In the same way that Mandrake can be poisonous, Bryony can be, too. Its love and fertility-drawing abilities aren't as good as they should be, but bryony has its own skills.

This is a good idea:

1. Take your money out of your wallet at night.

2. Stack it and put a bryony root (or part of one) on top to help it grow.

3. In the morning, return the money to your wallet and do it again if you need to.

There is a Buckeye spell that works.

Buckeyes have been used as money-making charms for a long time. One of the most well-known was to drill a hole in a buckeye, fill the hole with mercury, and then seal it. Mercury is very poisonous, and this spell gives you a lot of chances to hurt yourself. Instead, try this less dangerous but still magical option.

1. Add magnetic sand, Money Drawing Powder, Fast Luck Oil, and bergamot essential oil to a bowl. Mix well.

2. Use it on the buckeye.

3. Roll the buckeye toward you with either a new or old dollar bill in your hand.

4. Use crimson thread to tie it while you picture and make knots.

5. Use the rest of the paste to make two little green candles.

6. Place these candles next to each other on a tray that has been dusted with Money Drawing Powder so that they glow together.

When you put the buckeye in the middle of the candles, turn on the lights. Then your charm will start to work.

Spell of the Charm of the Buckeye

Conjure bag: Carry a buckeye and two big coins in the bag, and anoint it with money-drawing oils every day.

A spell for Buckwheat

People say that buckwheat is a good way to get rich. In the past, Japanese goldsmiths used dough made from buckwheat to catch gold dust as they worked. Culinary ways to use buckwheat's magical money-collecting powers are very popular. When you do culinary magic, think of the picture of the old witch stirring her cauldron and muttering and murmuring. Do the same thing when you make the meal, not just when you eat it. Over a pot of boiling buckwheat, whisper your goal.

He has magical money abilities that are at their best on New Year's Eve (or any other New Year's Eve; the point is that it's a threshold, not an exact date). At midnight on New Year's Eve, try eating noodles made from wheat, or pancakes made from wheat. This will bring good luck to your next year.

Cure Poverty with the Buckwheat Poverty Cure Spell

A clear glass dish is the best way to mix buckwheat hulls with dried basil and parsley, as well as salt and pepper. Keep this in the kitchen to keep money from coming in.

Spell for Attracting Good Fortune

Some individuals have a strong belief in good fortune. Others, on the other hand, rely on chance, and some people argue that things happen by chance, rejecting that a lucky break is dependent on us. Without considering the various perspectives on luck, it is difficult to deny that, on many occasions, our actions and will, combined with a set of facts - which may or may not be the result of chance - cause things to end up or turn out as we expected or, at the very least, that opportunities appear.

Continue reading if you've ever wondered what to do to be fortunate or whether there's a spell to alter our fate. We know certain rituals to attract good luck, whether in love or in other areas of your life, at OneHowTo.com. Take heed!

How to Attract Good Love Luck

If you want to attract the affection of a man or a woman, we may do the following ritual. We will craft a spell that will assist us in finding that individual, facilitating crossroads and allowing us to locate each other more swiftly. Furthermore, by doing so, we will be driving away loneliness, which may not have been with us till now.

This ceremony must be performed the week after the full moon to attract excellent beings in love. On the day of the full moon, instead of casting spells, strive to develop personally and engage in introspective exercises. On the contrary, if we perform this magic during a waxing moon, its effects will be amplified. Finally, before we go into how to do this ritual to improve your luck, keep in mind that Friday is the day of Venus, the goddess of love and beauty.

We'll need cinnamon sticks, a black marker, and red ribbon, ideally silk. We take three uncut cinnamon sticks and write our name on one and the name of the person we wish to attract on the other. We finish the spell by drawing a heart and the symbol of infinity on the remaining branch, therefore transmitting our wish for everlasting love. Tie the three twigs together with red silk ribbon and put them in a drawer away from direct sunlight. After a month, you must take them from the location where you stored them and bury them underground, for example, in the soil of a houseplant or in the garden soil.

Also, don't be afraid to know everything on the stones to attract love, as they may be useful in boosting your love fate.

How to Attract Financial Luck

If you desire greater luck when it comes to raising your money, there are several rituals that might aid you. In this area, we will introduce you to several rituals that can help you attract good luck and increase your finances.

Money-drawing ritual

This is one of the easiest rituals to do if we want to be really fortunate when it comes to filling our pockets. You will need 6 golden candles and a little amount of olive oil to carry it out. On a Sunday when the moon is waxing, light the candles and massage them with olive oil to keep the golden sheen of the candles from flaking off. After that, light the candles in one or more candle holders. Leave them on for an hour before turning them off. Repeat this technique six days in a row. Gold represents riches and wealth, while olive oil boosts the spell's efficacy and will assist us in achieving our aim.

Lottery Ritual

If the lottery is approaching or you have already purchased a ticket, this ritual will assist you in attracting good luck and increasing your chances of winning. We will require one of the elements with the strongest symbols of fortune for our ritual: the clover. You may be able to acquire a few if you have a garden at home. If you do not have a garden, you may go to a place where there is greenery and take some. Set three white candles in a triangle on a table and place the clovers in the middle. Ideally, no more than three clovers should be placed. Light the lights three times and repeat: "Bring good fortune with the strength of three, multiplying my wealth." Now all you have to do is hope that luck is on your side.

Finally, having plants to attract money is another excellent strategy. In this manner, you may increase your chances of attracting riches.

Home Rituals to Attract Good Luck

Our home is where we normally spend most of our time. Feeling at ease in our own environment is crucial, and we may strive to attract positive energies to create a nice atmosphere. We sometimes feel as though bad energy is flowing through our home, and we are not at ease. As a result, if you want to attract positive vibes while also feeling at ease at home, you may rely on the following ritual, which will also attract good luck. These luck-changing rituals are quite easy and may be completed in a matter of minutes.

Incense ritual to invoke good luck

This commodity has been utilized in religious rituals since ancient times since it was connected with magical properties that enabled spells to be performed. As a result, incense is one of the most often employed ingredients to generate good luck in many domains. In the case of the house, this product will not only clean it, but it will also help us create a nice atmosphere by emitting a pleasant odor. To do this, we may choose our favorite incense, fire it in the location where we wish to ward off negative energies, and allow it to burn. You may also burn incense and enter the various places to be cleansed. When a powerful scent fills your house, you will notice what a nice experience it is. These are some of the incenses we recommend for attracting good luck:

• African musk Assists in achieving more environmental harmony.

• Eucalyptus One of the most popular due to its excellent aroma, which aids in the cleansing of the home of negative energies that block bad luck. Its wonderful odor is soothing, and it will contribute to the overall pleasantness of the house.

• Sandalwood This incense has a flowery and exotic perfume that can help purify the home and remove any negative vibes that may be present.

If you want to learn more about this issue, you may watch a video in this post where we explain how to cleanse your house of bad energy.

Recommendations for obtaining good fortune

It is not enough to just follow rituals to attract good luck when we want to accomplish anything, whether it be love, money, or well-being. It is vital for us to become engaged and use our energies to the best of our abilities. It is vital to deposit trust, desire, and hope, fully believing in what we want to attract or accomplish. As a result, our mindset must shift in order to attract good luck rather than repel it, creating negative energy. Knowing how to open and activate the chakras is a fantastic method to redirect our energy in a beneficial direction. In this approach, we will develop inner calm and well-being, which will influence how we draw pleasant energies.

Conclusion

I hope you enjoyed reading this book as I enjoyed writing this book. There is a lot to be concerned about in our contemporary society, from the global (climate change, political instability) to the personal (a toxic ex, cyber bullying) level of concern. If you live in a stressful environment, spell crafting may assist you in finding comfort. This book will provide you with the skills you need to take care of your own defense in both the spirit and physical realms.

This book contains many spells for protection and defense, as well as a glossary of protective symbols, stones, and other objects to keep on hand. It can assist you in cleaning your room and casting out old negative energies, creating a protective and peace-preserving bubble around yourself while riding the bus, deflecting grumpiness and negativity from people you work with, and much more besides.

Two Special Gifts For You

Kitchen Witchery Ebook

The Guide to Discover ALL the Secret Powers of Foods and Herbs. Unlock the Great Magical Potential of your Spells by Introducing Magic into your Kitchen!

DOWNLOAD your guide for free or print it in PDF format

Spells & Rituals Template

Keep track of all your rituals with this magical template

DOWNLOAD your template for free or print it in PDF format

Printed in Great Britain
by Amazon

35866477R00086